© Mark Dennis Maurer 2020

Cabo San Lucas, BCS MEXICO

© Master of the Sales Universe

All rights reserved

*Fair use disclaimer "this book contains copyrighted material the use of which has not always been specifically authorized by the copyright owner"

Master of the Sales Universe

Applying the natural laws of the universe to create a dynamic sales career

Author: Mark D Maurer

When you turn the final page of this book, finish the last sentence and reflect intently on all the valuable content, you will have permanently shifted the paradigm of your sales career forever. Consistency in high performance can be achieved despite any current (though temporary) personal situations or challenges through understanding the natural laws of the universe.

The selling techniques described in the Master of the Sales Universe are designed to flow with the natural order of life to achieve a less resistant and extremely effective sales process. In each chapter there are many questions presented to the reader, which are purposefully left open in order for the audience to reflect and analyze the concepts independently. Critical thinking will allow each reader to come to their own conclusions on how they will implement those concepts into their personal success recipe.

When you understand how the world in which we live in functions and the laws that govern everything in existence, you can navigate through your victories and challenges with a new level of gratitude. You will learn that being grateful for the challenges in your life allows you to have dominion over them.

The purpose of this book and why you should read it continually over your sales career is to provide a concise guideline of the core laws of the universe and how understanding these laws will provide you with stability through all possible situations in your vocation.
If you choose, you can become a Master of your Sales Universe and it is the author's intention and the purpose of this book to provide you with the proper tools to make it possible.

The author has been a leading sales professional in the timeshare and fractional industry for over 20 years. Timeshare styled presentations require the entire sales process, from start to finish, be completed in as little as 90 minutes. "A short cycle covert close" which is equivalent to walking a tightrope while selling, with little room for error.

No matter if your sales process requires immediate action from your customer or requires multiple meetings to close, the irrefutable laws that you will master from these pages will allow you to be grateful and confident with each opportunity presented.

The Author did not create the universal laws however, the author has applied the knowledge of these laws to have a long lasting and fulfilling sales career and believes that can be replicated or surpassed by those whom desire to expand, grow and elevate themselves to higher levels of consciousness, civility, effectiveness and happiness.

"Man is always the master, even in his weaker and most abandoned state; but in his weakness and degradation he is the foolish master who misgoverns his "household." When he begins to reflect upon his condition, and to search diligently for the Law upon which his being is established, he then becomes the wise master, directing his energies with intelligence, and fashioning his thoughts to fruitful issues. Such is the conscious master, and man can only thus become by discovering within himself the laws of thought; which discovery is totally a matter of application, self analysis, and experience." James Allen

Table of Contents:

1. THE LAW OF VIBRATION
Everything that exists is energy constantly vibrating on a quantified frequency

2. THE LAW OF ATTRACTION
Energies of the same frequency attract each other

3. THE LAW OF TRANSMUTATION
Transform thought energy into envisioned results

4. THE LAW OF RHYTHM
Change is continually constant and life is in cycles

5. THE LAW OF POLARITY
Everything that exists has a spectrum of extremes

6. THE LAW OF GESTATION
Everything manifests through an incubation process

7. THE LAW OF RELATIVITY
Everything IS, until it is compared to something else

8. THE LAW OF CAUSE AND EFFECT
Every action has an equal and opposite reaction

9. THE LAW OF GENDER
Everything has masculine and feminine components

10. THE LAW OF ACTION
Energy does not move without definite action

11. THE LAW OF CORRESPONDENCE
Connection exists between conscious and subconscious

12. THE LAW OF THE CONNECTED UNIVERSE

Everything in the universe is connected through energy and origin

"One is first a student to become a master; a master is always a student; when a master ceases to grow a master one ceases to be"
Author-Mark Maurer

CHAPTER 1. THE LAW OF VIBRATION

Everything that exists is energy constantly vibrating on a quantified frequency

Think of yourself as a broadcast tower. What vibrational frequency do you want to broadcast to your spouse, family, coworkers and, of course, your customers? Is your broadcast something that people will want to listen, follow or be persuaded by? Your energy and vibrational frequency show up in your body language, tone of voice, eye contact and nonverbal communication. You are always broadcasting, even when you are not consciously aware of it. You are a walking and talking spiritual being comprised of or represented in energy. Your thoughts, for example, carry waves of energy through a frequency. That energy can then change forms through transmutation, like water to ice. Your thoughts can transform into a physical reality when energy is focused in a specific direction. In fact, everyone and everything that exists is comprised of energy. From the molecular level to the objects as they appear in our personal realities, everything is vibrating energy. Inevitability, there are countless frequencies of vibration.

As a sales professional, you will want to observe that all things in existence (including your customers) are vibrating on a frequency that is parallel to their current consciousness. If your customer is in a bad mood from something that occurred before your interaction, that vibration could carry over into your sales meeting. Being able to recognize a person or group's vibrational energy can provide the guide on how to raise that vibrational energy to a much higher frequency by using emotional questions, humor or situational techniques to change their mood and their frequency.

*Try this simple experiment... Have two people from opposite ends of a room (with eyes closed or blind folded) slowly move towards each other (others should be helping to make sure no one gets hurt). As the two people get closer to one another, ask that as soon as one senses the others presence they should stop and go no further. Undoubtedly, each time it is done the two people will always feel the others presence before fully reaching each other. This is because, though without sight, you can feel someone's vibrational energy without actually seeing the other person.

Have you ever been in public and met someone you instantly felt a very different vibrational frequency than yours? Have you ever been around someone for a few minutes and felt the need to escape? This person's vibrational energy is on a much different frequency than yours. Have you ever had a customer that you could not communicate with no matter how you tried to explain yourself?

All people, including your customers, are constantly vibrating forms of energy and their conscious thoughts are vibrating on a certain frequency. So, the question becomes, how can you take this understanding of vibrational frequency to create greater sales success?

If every person is vibrational energy and broadcasting on a certain frequency, then it requires you, as sales professional, to learn how to raise your customer's vibrational frequency into a high level. High emotional frequencies include peace, joy, love, reason and willingness. Creating a broadcast that can elevate your customer's emotional state through frequency is more effective than which words you use. As an example, what happens when a customer reaches a positive high frequency? On the contrary, what normally happens when a customer is in a low frequency state, like anger, fear, grief, or apathy? Will your customer feel good enough to purchase <u>right now</u> if they are <u>not</u> in a positive vibrational frequency? The answer is obvious, so the question becomes how can YOU create a positive broadcast frequency?

Enthusiasm for your product will create a positive broadcast frequency…

Belief and faith in your product will create a positive broadcast frequency…

Service first sales mentality will create a positive broadcast frequency…

Enthusiasm is the first step to creating a frequency bridge into your prospect's consciousness. Enthusiasm is deep rooted in gratitude and can be maximized by creating a list of the things that you are most grateful in relation to your company and product. With repetition you can create a career foundation constructed in gratitude. This grateful state of mind projects a high vibrational frequency that your customers will react to in a positive way. The result is active customer participation which opens the door to their active listening and creates a positive audience that get excited to be involved in the process.

Belief and faith in your product or service, results in your customer trusting your sales presentation's integrity by sensing your sincerity. Your sincerity is communicated through your tone of voice, extended eye contact, body language, facial expressions and all non-verbal communicators. Conviction develops from your thinking and becomes one of your most valuable assets. Conviction is without fear and unwavering energy and when you are able to develop conviction with your product you are able to be bold and unapologetic in pursuit of the sale.

Service first sales mentality is a reflection of your dedication and commitment to excellence. Consider the Law of Cause and Effect...if you are servicing your own needs and not the needs of your customer there is an effect which will occur which will result in a win-loss scenario. Win-loss relationships always end up in failure. Service first sales mentality is a pursuit of a win-win result in which all parties are benefactors through comprehension and balance. Consider the words of Ralph Waldo Emerson, "The purpose of life is not to be happy. It is to be useful, to be honorable, to be compassionate, to have it make some difference that you have lived and lived well". Having a service first sales mentality will serve YOU well and will provide you a champion's philosophy.

Additionally, mastering the law of vibration is key to interpreting meaning in the world around you, understanding the flow of energy, and creating relationships (including your customer relationships) through broadcasting your tonality at a high vibrational frequency. The results will include an elevation of your customer's mood and a heightening of their vibrational frequency to a fully engaged state.

    Note that there will be times that no matter what you attempt to do, you are unable to change the customer's frequency. In these times, give your customer something to read or look at and excuse yourself. Find a place to gather your composure, and think of a person or place that makes you <u>feel</u> really happy (like going to your own Happy Gilmor's 'happy place') and return to your customer when your frequency has been adjusted. Often times, when we remove our egos and recognize the law of vibration at work it is possible to persuade a buyer, whom was adamantly opposed, by simply changing your thinking, tone of voice or vibrational frequency (emotional state) of your energy.

    Thought vibrational frequency, and its physical effects, are very real and scientifically proven. [1]**Dr. Masaru Emoto's** *HIDDEN MESSAGES IN WATER* revealed that conditions, music and human thought vibrations can alter the molecular state of water. The experiments determined that, positive or negative thought vibrations actually alter the water's physical appearance upon freezing, thus proving the existence of thought vibrations and their physical effects in the transmutation of water. Geometric shapes were captured in the frozen water with vast differences between the positive and negative messaging. Human bodies consist of 70% water, so it is easy to see that your vibrational energy can affect every facet of your life. Often affecting your physicality, choice of words, your posture, and your overall vibrational broadcast. Emoto's experiment also confirms that when energy trans-mutates, the new form is affected by the frequency. Therefore, when the water changed to ice, it's appearance and form were altered from the positive and negative messages (which carry an energy frequency). Dr. Emoto concluded that, "Words are the vibrations of nature. Therefore, beautiful words create beautiful nature. Ugly words create ugly nature. This is the root of the universe." This will be further explored in Chapter 3, where you will learn to take your powerful positive energy and transform it into a shining light of enthusiasm and gratitude that will change your level of performance on a permanent basis.

In 2014, my kids and I decided to make our own version of Dr. Emoto's experiment. My daughter, son and I wrote positive and negative messages (smiley faces, frowns and a variety empowering words) on plastic cups. We filled each cup with soil and a seed. Each cup displayed either positive or negative messages. We wanted to see if the vibrational frequency of the messages would have any effect on our veggies. The 'happiest cup' was a cucumber plant that my daughter adorned with positive messages. We were in astonishment while 'q-key' yielded more than 100 cucumbers, while NONE of the negative messaged seeds grew or yielded any fruit or vegetable.

What frequency are your messages and communication being broadcast from? Each thought you have is a thought vibrational frequency or a thought seed. As **Napoleon Hill** once famously wrote, "thoughts are things" and indeed they are. Nothing exists that did not start first as a seed. This will be further explored in the Law of Gestation Chapter.

Tonality of voice is directly related to frequency and the frequency of your seeds will yield accordingly. For example, in November 23, 2015 the ₂University of Southern California released a study which took couples in counseling and analyzed their sessions with a computer algorithm. The algorithm was able to identify the couples that would improve their relationships with greater accuracy than the professional human experts that were working with the couples directly. The algorithm was able to predict the couple's probable viability based on their tone of voice alone. The algorithm was nearly 79 percent accurate in the study. "Words can deceive, but tone of voice cannot", the Science News article concluded. This is more underlying evidence that our frequency cannot be faked by our words, but can be felt with our tone of voice.

Apply this discovery to your daily sales approach and you will see that it is, in fact, true. Your tonality is the pitch of your frequency. It's not what you say, instead it is how you say it that communicates the real information. What tone of voice do you use when persuading a child? Have you ever detected someone's tone as cynical? How is your tone of voice when you are greeting a friend?

What would happen if you greeted your next customer with the tone of voice you use for your best friend? Is it possible you would more easily connect? What if right before you meet with your customers you felt like you were about to talk with your best friend? Would your tone of voice and frequency be different? This is a great technique and works exceptionally well. Think of someone you really get excited to see and envision them. Feel the emotions you may have when you are with them. Shift that energy into your immediate frequency and enter your meeting with that feeling and your tonality will mirror that of your frequency.

In 1981, ₃biologist Helene Grimal partnered up with music composer Fabien Maman. They wanted to study the effect of music on living cells. The experiment was conducted with a camera and microscope. Living cancer cells were exposed to musical instruments (guitar, xylophone, gong) set at a 30-40 decibels. The experiment was set for 20 minutes per session, but the cancer cells exploded, under the microscope, at the **fourteen**-minute mark. Maman and Grimal, then repeated the experiment using a human voice instead of musical instruments. Astonishingly, the cancer cells exploded in only **nine** minutes with the human voice. It proved that the frequency of the human voice can destroy living cancer cells. Later, in a third experiment, with two female breast cancer patients, Grimal and Maman used human voice frequency, for 3 hours a day, to eliminate the cancer cells from the two female patients. Conclusion, the human voice and its tone and frequency can have tremendous effects all the way down to the cellular vibrational level. So, how do you create a tone of voice that can have greater impact?

The evidence seems to point that our state of mind will have impact on our tone of voice. Grateful attitudes create harmonious and lively frequency energy. Your voice is a representation of your entire energy force or the sound culmination of your being. Your tone will communicate your frequency.

    Body language, meaning all interpreted messages derived from visual physicality, is inherent to vibrational energy. Body language can provide a vast amount of information to the message receiver. If everything is energy, then that energy has a physical manifestation, and therefore we can derive much information from any object and its subsequent body language. Mastering the interpretation of body language and knowing how to send the most positive messages from your body language are crucial in all in person sales meetings. The law of vibration provides us a guide to align our energy with what we want to attract. So, consider how your body language is providing clues to your customer about your intent and vibrational frequency just as their body language is communicating their interest level and focus on your sales presentation. Have you ever completely read someone's attitude by just looking at their body language? The reason is our non-verbal communication **speaks volumes**.

    Take [4]**Albert Mehrabian's** 7-38-55 RULE and apply it to the law of vibration. Mehrabians's rule states that communication between speaker and audience is demonstrated by 7% literal (word) content,

38% is tonality and volume, and 55% is body language content. This rule is an amazingly revealing and, of course, reinforces the deeper explanation behind what is really going on between people communicating. MASTERING BODY LANGUAGE is key to creating a lasting sales career. If you want to work on your craft you can start by analyzing how you stand, sit, walk and present information with your customers. Is your stance open? Do you walk with confidence and purpose? Do you sit directly facing your customer with your chest and heart exposed to them? How effective are you with using hand gestures? Do you guide your customer's eyes towards the direction you would like them to look? Are your movements animated? Does your body language exude stability? By first appearance, would you want to do business with yourself?

    Does your eye contact stay intent on your customer when they are asking you buying questions? Does your body language explain to your customer that you are fully engaged? What are you doing to communicate with non-verbal methods? Are you raising and accentuating your eye brows to create excitement (like an excited and innocent child)? Are you moving your head ever so slightly in a positive nodding movement? How do you feel when you are with someone that is constantly smiling? Does it encourage you to smile also? If you are familiar with the concept of mirroring and matching your customer, then consider why it actually works. It is a frequency connector. It allows the customer to perceive a similarity with you and will assist you in finding a wavelength frequency to communicate with them.

Non-verbal communication (7/38/55 rule) is an area that any Master of the Sales Universe will want to spend much time and energy focused on. My suggestion is to start with your own vibrational energy which will positively affect your non-verbal efforts. GRATITUDE IS KEY. When you are truly grateful for your life and everything in it, that vibration will carry over (with honesty and intent) into your actual body language. If your product makes you excited and you truly believe that your product will have a great benefit to your customer, that belief will carry over through all your forms of communication. You could be a very gifted speaker, but without conviction the message will be flat and unimpressive. Are you grateful to be involved with your product or service? Are you vibrating on a "service first" frequency? Service first frequency translates to your customer as, "this person understands me (or us)". Therefore, there is no more powerful tool for you to wield as a Master of the sales universe, than vibrating in a grateful state.

You may have heard this said as having a good attitude, but a good attitude is based on a gratitude for what one has when energy is focused on positive aspects. Those that focus their energy on lack (ex: if this were to occur then I would be happy...) and what they don't have, will vibrate on a lower frequency and often the customer will pick up that vibration through tonality or body language when the words are communicating something different.

One of my mentors, Terry Harker, changed my life with this simple way to stay in a state of gratitude... Imagine as a parent, that you give a gift to your child. Imagine that your child upon receiving the gift becomes very upset, because the item they wanted was a different color or a different style and in turn cry and complain upon receiving the gift. How will you feel as a parent? Would you want to give your child more gifts if that is how they are going to react? Now, imagine that your child has become very happy and excited upon receiving the gift. Their reaction tells you how elated they truly are. How will that make you feel as a parent? Would it make you happy to know that your child is so pleased with what they have received? Would you want to give that child more gifts because of their positive reaction?

Regardless of your religious beliefs, there is a creator to this vibrational field of energy we live in and the more grateful you are of what you have received and what you believe is coming for you, the more that vibrational energy will be rewarded in the material world. Being grateful, each day you wake up, is the most effective recipe to becoming your best representation in the vibrational universe.

*"**Master your vibrational frequency**"*

"I would maintain that thanks are the highest form of thought; and that gratitude is happiness doubled by wonder." G.K. Chesterton

"Be content with what you have; rejoice in the way things are. When you realize there is nothing lacking, the whole world belongs to you" Lao Tzu

"I will give thanks to you, LORD, with all my heart; I will tell of all your wonderful deeds." Psalms 9:1

2. THE LAW OF ATTRACTION

Energies of the same frequency attract each other

The law of attraction seems to be a subject that has been widely explored over recent years. So much so that it seemed daunting to take this chapter on so early into the book. However, the Laws of vibration and attraction are so closely related that I felt compelled to keep them together in consecutive chapters.

A great description of the law of attraction and how people magnetize their thought vibrational frequencies comes from the classic, *AS A MAN THINKETH*, "Men do not attract that which they want, but that which they are. Their whims, fancies, and ambitions are thwarted at every step, but their inmost thoughts and desires are fed with their own food, be it foul or clean. The "divinity that shapes our ends" is in ourselves; it is our very self. Only himself manacles man: thought and action are the gaolers of Fate—they imprison, being base; they are also the angels of Freedom—they liberate, being noble. Not what he wishes and prays for does a man get, but what he justly earns. His wishes and prayers are only gratified and answered when they harmonize with his thoughts and actions."

We attract what we are focusing our thought vibrational energy on. The universe is energy. Your thoughts are energy. Energy moves through frequency waves. You can't listen to your favorite radio station without tuning into the exact frequency to get their signal and for exactly the same reasons you cannot receive your favored results without tuning your thought vibrations to the desired attainment through frequency.

Case in point, in 2016 the Diamante sales team had a three-month sales contest. The winner of the contest would win a week vacation in a multi-million-dollar home or condo in North America with flights included for 2 persons. I brought home and taped the contest page to my bedroom mirror. I had determined that I would win the contest to take my kids somewhere special (just the three of us). Without going in to details, there were some marital problems and my kids and I were no longer living together full time. When they came to visit, I showed them the contest page and told them, "Daddy is going to win this sales contest, so where do you want to go?" My son and daughter decided on New York City. I promised them we would go and stay in something spectacular and that I would win the contest.

For three months I looked at the contest page and thought of the three of us having an amazing time in the Big Apple. We looked at helicopter tour information online and checked out apps that have Broadway show times. I also spoke with people I knew from the New York area for restaurant recommendations. I was convinced that I would win even though the contest was not cut and dry.

The contest rules consisted of receiving tickets for each sale and at the end of the 3 months there would be a dinner and at the dinner there would be a raffle to determine the winner. The best option was to have more tickets than anyone else in order to have the best odds of winning. So, even if someone did have the most sales (most tickets) there was still the possibility that they would not win.

I was convinced I would win, despite the rules, and my performance those months reflected that belief. In a sales department with many great performers I managed to earn more tickets than anyone for the dinner event, but that did not guarantee winning the trip it only gave me better odds. At the moment of the ticket drawing, a random woman was walking by and was asked to draw a ticket from the basket. The woman reached inside the basket and handed the ticket over to the sale director in order to match up the name...

When my name was called, it seemed that I had already imagined it having been done. It was overwhelming and exciting because I had illustrated to my kids that the Law of Attraction works in our lives because of the focus of thought vibrations. The idea of winning the contest had become a recognized frequency for me. Focused energy is a cause and its effect will be attracting other energies that are vibrating on the same frequency. It's because there are countless frequencies and each frequency can be tapped into if you have the frequency code just like calling your friend on the cell phone. If you are broadcasting on the frequency of what you wish to attain it will be attracted to you through vibrational frequency. Once you've dialed in on exactly what you want, there will be an incubation period before you receive it. This process is covered in the Law of Gestation chapter, so keep reading.

Where you focus your energy, in your sales career, is where your sales career will be. If it is your desire to be the number one sales person in your company or if you are selling real estate part time and you want to maximize the time you spend working, it always comes down to where you are focusing your attention. Is your attention on growth? Is your focus on certain goals? Is your focus on a co-worker who is doing better than you? Is your focus on the weekend? Is your focus on next month? Where are your thoughts through-out the day?

One of my mentors, Chris Shryack, has a company called Performance with Power. Chris is very passionate about helping his clients reach new heights in their personal and business lives. He calls it full spectrum life. Chris has 4 things the he does every time he's about to go to work, whether speaking in front of a crowd or doing a one-on-one phone call with a client, which are the following:

-Take a few minutes to get prepared
-Ask yourself, how can I stay fully engaged?
-Emotional willingness
-Always expect a break through

Applying these 4 action steps daily, right before going to work, will create an alignment with the law of attraction.

Why would you want to take a *few minutes to prepare yourself*? Imagine that your thoughts are laser focused on your objectives for the day. If you are not taking a few minutes to meditate and clear your mind of negative thought vibrations before you meet with your prospect, it is likely you are unprepared to perform at your highest possible level. How does that relate to attraction? Are you attracting the best situation possible each day?

How can you stay fully engaged? I love this step because it is a great reminder of how you can focus your thought vibrations, throughout the entire sales process, on the outcome. Or as [23]**Dr. Covey** from *THE 7 HABITS OF HIGHLY EFFECTIVE PEOPLE* would say, "begin with the end in mind". The law of attraction is very much determined by these thought patterns. If you are fully committed to stay engaged in the sales process to the very end, then it is likely that your thought vibrations are not blurry or somewhere else from the task at hand.

When you include your *emotional willingness*, you are creating an 'openness to possibilities' and announcing that you are ALL IN. You are here to serve and spend whatever time it takes to be of service. It is more difficult to attract like energy when you are closed to possibilities.

Being open to any and all possibilities is where true break throughs happen and that's why Chris believes that by always going into your next sales meeting with the *expectation of a break through*, you are much more likely to experience something amazing. That's not by luck or by chance, it's because you are a comprised of energy and you are tuned into a frequency that is expecting something special to happen. Imagine going to your job each day expecting something 'big' to happen. How would you feel about going to the office each day knowing that something special will happen when you're there? How will that effect your vibrational broadcast frequency? Is it possible you will attract more special and exciting situations, if you simply believe that they're going to occur to you? I recommend you experiment with this vibrational frequency exercise because it will develop your vibrational belief system. You will be amazed with the little daily break throughs that you attract. What do you want to attract into your vocation today?

    When people say "live with passion", how does that translate to these universal laws? Passion, or extreme desire, is an intense and focused thought vibrational frequency. Your thoughts can become consumed with a certain subject matter and grow in its intensity. Masters of the sales universe will learn to take their passion for sales and convert that vibrational frequency to all areas of their endeavors. If you want to attract a certain type of customer then you will want to write down all the characteristics and attributes of your ideal prospect and then follow that up with your thought vibrations. You can get as detailed as you'd like. Once you are ready you can follow that up with meditation where you see yourself with those customers signing an agreement. Believe that there are customers, exactly like you've described, waiting to do business with you in a win-win agreement. Set your intention and subsequent frequency to begin the attraction process.

You want to acquire a larger selling region than you currently have now, then you will want to write out and describe the ideal region of your choice. You want to raise your closing percentage by 10%, then you will apply energy to learn and vision yourself with the higher percentage. You will want to write down the exact closing percentage you want and see your name appearing next to the percentage and include an obtainable target date that it will occur within to keep your energy focused towards the goal.

Attraction between two magnets cannot be visibly observed, however, it works whether you believe it or not. There are magnets large enough to move heavy metal objects without effort. YOU are also a magnet and you don't have to visibly see it to know that it works. The law of attraction illustrates how things that are vibrating at the same frequency are attracted to each other, like magnets. When you hold a thought in your mind and transfer your energy to maintaining that thought, it will in fact appear to you in its physical form. This means that whatever you focus your thoughts on you will attract, even if it is something you don't desire. **Earl Nightingale** revealed in the THE STRANGEST SECRET that, "a man's life becomes what he thinks about".

Therefore, you will want to guard your thoughts because they are your vibrational currency. It will serve you well to begin being impeccable with your thoughts and words. Your thoughts and words create paradigms that set limits to your attraction power. For example:

I can't do that.

I don't think that's possible.

I'll never be.

I'm too old.

Your thought management is key. Your thoughts will determine the outcome. If you don't think it's possible then you are very unlikely to realize it. These frequency blockers or paradigms, limit your belief system and therefore, limit what you are able to attract. When you use words like; **need, must,**

have to, should, have got to, your frequency is broadcasting a lack of abundance.

"I have to make a sale today…"

"I must get this done now…"

"I need to do this…"

All of these statements are broadcasting that you have no choice or option and your frequency is a lack of abundance. What do you believe you will be attracting with that frequency? When you use words like; ***want, will, get to, choose to, I'm privileged to***, your frequency is broadcasting that life is abundant and you can choose what you want.

"I want to do this now…"

"I will make sure it gets done…"

"I choose to stay late…"

"I get to enjoy…"

All of these statements begin from a freedom of choice perspective or what Chris Shryack calls *emotional willingness*. Which perspective and frequency do you want to broadcast to your customers? Can you feel the underlining vibrational frequency of gratitude? You don't have to do anything except what you want and choose to do. [6]**Deepak Chopra** says, "The law of giving is very simple. If you want joy, give joy. If love is what you seek, offer love. If you crave material affluence, help others become prosperous."

Masters of the Sales Universe realize that in order to receive more they will first give more. There are many good sales people that believe if they help others improve it will be to their own detriment, however, that is not how the Law of Attraction works. Focusing on lack will bring lack while focusing on abundance will bring more abundance, so feel free to be helpful with your co-workers because it 'sharpens your saw' in the process.

How does the principle 'give to receive' relate to service first vibrational frequency? What will you attract if your thought vibrations are focused on the needs of your customer? What will you attract if your thought vibrations are focused on your sales commission while you are engaged in the sales process? Can you see why protecting your thoughts is so important? What habits can you adopt to attract more of what you want out of your career?

How will you take responsibility for advancing your sales career? How will you create success from your passion? How has the law of attraction effected your sales career? What personal adjustments can you make to fully capitalize from your new understanding of the law of attraction? When should you begin?

"Master attracting what you desire"

"All things that you ask straightly, directly, from inside my name, you will be given. So far you have not done this". Jesus from the Gospel of Thomas

"You must make your future dream a present fact" Neville Goddard - The Power of Awareness

"Do not be deceived, God is not mocked; for whatever a man sows, this he will also reap" Galatians 6:7

"At the center of your being you have the answer; you know who you are and you know what you want" Lao Tzu

3. THE LAW OF TRANSMUTATION

All energy moves in and out of physical form

Albert Einstein once said, "Energy cannot be created or destroyed, it can only be changed from one form to another". You will learn that you can transform you thought vibrational energy into your envisioned results. For example, water changes form to steam when the vibrational frequency is sped up and turns to ice when the vibrational frequency is slowed down. A plant is transformed from living organism to a converted energy source when consumed by an herbivore. A log in a fireplace turning from wood to ash is simply changing forms, or trans-mutating. The energy, that is the wood, exudes heat as it transforms to ash. Your thoughts are creative energy which you can also trans-mutate into its physical form.

Corporate sales director of Pueblo Bonito Resorts, Eric White, sums up well how the law of transmutation applies to sales, which is: **"The definition of a timeshare sales person is an individual with the ability to create interest in the concept of vacation ownership where no interest previously lied."**

Does that mean, that a sales person has to create something from nothing? How do you just create something? Is imagination important in creating sales interest? How do you take a new prospect with no established interest in your product, and create a new customer?

Every sale starts as a seed and through a process grows from an idea to a commitment to purchase. Energy is neither created nor destroyed, so the seed is energy drawn from your imagination and enthusiasm. An avocado seed will always yield avocado trees. Your thought vibrations, when applied as focused energy, can trans-mutate into **sales seeds** to be planted in the fertile soil of your client's mind. Would you like to know how you can trans-mutate energy into sales production?

I had a chance to meet Alan Muhlaley in 2014. Mr. Muhlaley, was the CEO of Ford Motor Company, at the time, and had previously been the CEO of Boeing. Arguably one of the best executives in America. When an opportunity opened, I asked him what he could share about creating success. His response was one that I will never forget. He said there are three items that are very important to creating success, which are, **"Vision, Strategy, and Trust in the Process".**

Apply this success formula to a sales presentation:

What is your **vision for this...**?

Day? Week? Year? Career?

How specific can you make your vision?

Why is it so important to be specific?

What is your **strategy** for your next sales meeting?

How will you accomplish your vision?

What will take priority in your life to accomplish this vision?

What will you sacrifice to replace with your vision?

What will you need to learn to reach your vision?

Who do you need to become to accomplish your vision?

    By staying committed to the vision and the strategy, we can **trust in the process** to yield our desired results. Deviate from the formula and chaos ensues. Here are a few rules that all sales people can apply to ensure that they are trusting in the process - **no shortcuts, follow all steps to the sale, never prejudge your**

client's potential and trust in the process till the end and then ask for the order one last time.

Now let's be very clear. This success formula is effective because of the law of trans-mutation. The vision is an energy seed, a **sales seed**. The 'vision' can be trans-mutated into the material reality with the application of (action) energy and unwavering persistence.

Apply the formula to your next sales meeting:

*Discover what the vision of your client's future looks like to them...

*Help them create a strategy that will be best suited to achieve their vision...

*Have unwavering persistence in the pursuit of their vision...

Transform thought vibration energy into a sale by trusting the process to the end. A Master of the Sales Universe can trans-mutate energy from discovering key information about their client with effective questions and transfer that visualization into their client's imagination. Think of the martial arts master who can transfer energy force (chi) unto their opposition without even touching them. In sales, you can transfer the 'vision' energy into creating **sales participation**, **active listening**, ***trying on the vision*** and finally by ***taking action***. Our positive thought vibrational energy (gratitude and enthusiasm) and unwavering persistence form a powerful energy stream which you can direct and transfer to your clients. For example, you can deliver your description of your customer enjoying their new purchase from their perspective, "you drive your new car up to the lake for the weekend, you pack some clothes and groceries and throw them in that spacious trunk, you entertain the kids on the way with a movie on the seat screens and you start enjoying your new family SUV while you drive up to the lake in safety and comfort". By the end of the description your customer has seen themselves driving to the lake with their new purchase and you have trans-mutated their vision with your assistance (putting them in the picture of ownership).

LOVE VIBRATION is an energy you can hold to create many splendid things in your life, including connecting with your customers. Conviction selling requires the seller to be completely in love and convinced with his or her product (or service). When you are completely in love with your product you will transfer that high-level frequency to your customer. Combine that love vibration with finding something that you genuinely love about your customer (there is always something special about every individual person – seek that in each customer and you will find a genuine appreciation for them) and that energy will transmit into a reciprocating energy from your customer. The law of reciprocation dictates that when someone genuinely is attracted to you, you will reciprocate the sentiment. You cannot dislike someone who you can feel genuinely likes you. How could you reject someone with such great taste? **Love vibration** also enhances each sales meeting because you hold a positive energy for your product and for the opportunity to meet a special and interesting person. How could you not be excited to go to work every day and introduce something you love to someone you have just fallen in love with? This is not romantic love (though I have married friends who met during a sales meeting), but a frequency connecting love. A kind of, "I really like this person!" or "what a neat couple, their lives are so interesting", type of love vibration. The law of the connected universe explains that all energy is connected to a source and we are all a part of this energy. In India and to those familiar with yoga, the word used to describe this notion is **Namaste**. It calls for us to recognize the connection we have to each person even if we don't share their same opinion. It's recognizing and appreciating their life force and their potential.

Take this philosophy into your daily sales meetings. Remove all social labels you may conclude from your first impressions of someone and be reminded that they are, just like you, only human. May I recommend looking at each person with a lens of namaste and see your client with a new and refreshed vision. Your clients, like you, are looking for acceptance, love and recognition of their achievements. Not only will this technique do wonders for your broadcast and frequency connecting, but it will enhance the entire world you live in. Respect and love reciprocate respect and love. Trans-mutating positive thought vibrations to those around you is how you can constantly recycle positive energy.

Conviction is belief. Belief is stored energy. Have you heard the saying, "the one with the most conviction wins"? The reason, trans-mutation of positive energy will subside the lesser negative energy. If you have unwavering conviction about your product and you master the ability to transfer that energy to your customer, you will perform at an extremely high level. This cannot be fake. Faking belief will not be effective because the vibration cannot be faked, no different than words do not convey the message as truthfully as tonality. You must believe to convert the non-believer.

Sales participation occurs when you combine conviction in your product with a service first sales vibration. **Active listening** begins to occur as your client becomes an active participant in the process. Your client will begin to open up about their true feelings, opinions or begin to ask "buying" questions regarding your product or service. This begins the manifestation of your sale. This is where the sales seed energy is transforming in to their vision. Stay the course and trust in the process as your client begins to take mental possession of your product. Conception of that energy trans-mutates into your clients **trying on the vision**. Your client's conception of a future with your product in their life and their vision of whom and how they will enjoy it, is how the sales seed energy transforms into your client's thought vibrations.

Sales is a transference of thought energy (emotion). Why is enthusiasm such a desired trait of sales people? How does transferring enthusiasm (positive concentrated energy) create sales momentum? Is enthusiasm simply a trans-mutation of positive energy?

The law of trans-mutation occurs during every sales transaction. Clearly, to be a Master of the Sales Universe you will need to master the trans-mutating of enthusiastic thought energy into specific customized sales seeds. Applying enthusiastic positive energy and unwavering persistence with a structured strategy, that is consistent with your vibrational frequency, you can follow through and trust in the process until the energy fully transforms into your customer's vision.

Trans-mutating negative energy can be prevented and it starts with guarding your thoughts. Personal issues, finances, marital problems, etc. are not allowed into your broadcast vibrational energy during the trans-mutation process or their negative effects will appear as evident as Dr. Emoto's water to ice experiments. Problematic negative energy has no place in your work space. A surgeon should have a sterile environment to perform surgery, a farmer should remove all weeds before planting their crops, and a sales professional should be in a positive vibrational frequency before attempting to trans-mutate that energy.

Taking action, for your new client, will begin once the sales seed energy has fully changed forms. The transference can sometimes occur very quickly, especially if your client had already thought, at some point, of buying a similar product to yours. Often assuming your client will purchase, you can simply say, "here's the order form please fill out the information and we'll get this started". Sometimes that is all it takes for the trans-mutation to have occurred and the clients start filling out the forms. Occasionally the customer says, "are we doing this?", to their partner or spouse and will get confirmation to start filling out the forms.

There will be times, even though you've done everything accordingly well, your prospect does not take action. Fear is the general reason your prospect does not move forward. Fear of the unknown is normally a deep-rooted vibration which freezes many from wanting to make a poor buying decision. Fear is an absence of faith. Fear is a low vibration frequency. If your client is overcome with fear they are not going to buy and if they somehow do buy, they are likely to try and rescind the agreement promptly thereafter. How is it possible to sell more frequently than you already do?

Learn ways to remove the fear from your prospect and replace it with faith. Selling is a transference of emotion. Objections are fears. Mastering the law of trans-mutation, you will broadcast thought vibrations on a high frequency and persuade through converting positive energy into customized sales seeds. Plus, you can neutralize any objection by replacing that fear vibration with faith. This includes the no money objection. People will go to great lengths to acquire the things they truly believe they want in their lives, so if your prospect has a strong enough desire, they will find a way to pay for it. How well you master the law of trans-mutation will determine how well you succeed in sales mastery.

"Master trans-mutating enthusiasm"

"Fire, after all, does not consume. It transmutates" Kaia Anderson

"Grapes must be crushed to make wine. Diamonds form under pressure. Olives are pressed to release oil. Seed grow in the dark. Whenever you feel crushed, under pressure, or in darkness, you're in a powerful place of transformation and transmutation. Trust the process." Lalah Delia

4. THE LAW OF RHYTHM

Change is continually constant and life is in cycles

"One of my main motivations to write this book, was to share this most important law to all those pursuing a sales career." Author

Everything has a natural life cycle. Over the course of a year the seasons change and the weather patterns with it. The weather conditions, around the world, are followed and tracked, but regardless of educated predictions and identified seasons, the weather can change quickly from what it was predicted to do. Growing up in Texas, the saying goes, "if you don't like the weather wait a few minutes because it will change".

Ocean conditions change very quickly. The tide rises and falls over the course of the day. The waves come in and then they push back out. The ocean conditions are always changing. There are websites dedicated to reading and following the ocean tides and despite that fact, the ocean movements are still unpredictable. The universe is a continual life cycle with countless shifting energies.

In 1852, author **Edward FitzGerald** wrote in his fable poem [7]SOLOMON'S SEAL, that when

King Solomon was asked to make a wise statement for the ages, that could apply to good times and bad, his response was, **"THIS TOO SHALL PASS"**. Truly one of the most accurate descriptions of the human experience ever made and to be a Master of the Sales Universe it will require you to embrace each moment because, **this too shall pass**.

What meaning does that have for you?

Wherever you may be in your sales career. Whether you are the current salesperson of the year for your sales organization or you had your worst performance in recent years and your reading this book to get your career back on track, the fact remains, change is constant. Life and all it's moving parts are always changing, so to get too attached to any particular thing will inevitably end with pain and negative recourse.

Complacency is the where people get caught up in this law. Without fully understanding these cycles, one could get frustrated with consistency. Many of us want to control outer factors which are beyond our control or influence.

Get too comfortable with your supervisor, then your supervisor is replaced and it can completely affect your results. Allow your success to go to your head and your ego will inflate with the words of other's praises and a few months later you're pulling your hair out asking yourself how will ever sell again. Realizing that the law of rhythm's flow is like the ocean tide you can choose to be the steady rock protruding from the water. Sometimes you will stand out big and tall for all to see and other times you are covered by the high tide and swirling surf, but no matter the water level you are solid and immovable. Mastery of the Law of Rhythm allows you to never get too high or too low with your thought vibrational energy because "this too shall pass".

    Do not allow your results, whatever they may have been recently, affect your thought vibrations. Being too elated when you make a sale trans-mutates into a self-serving vibrational broadcast and your customers will be turned off. Equally damaging is when you are in a sales slump and trans-mutating the self-serving sales vibration of lack or need. Either way, these extreme emotional states translate directly to our broadcast vibrational frequency and can take any good salesperson and turn them into an emotional roller coaster.

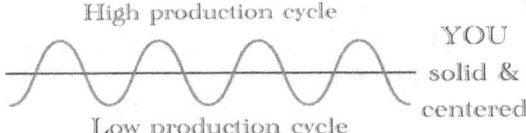

The beauty to embracing the Law of Rhythm is that you will actually enjoy all moments of your sales career and not just the glory. The sales career cycle is as follows:

*Constant learning during every cycle.

*On the high success cycle (you are kicking serious tail with high energy), you should record your sales meetings and keep a sales journal to document your successes. Take note of how you feel during this cycle, in order to duplicate that frequency for times when you are not in the high success zone.

*On the low production cycle (sucking wind with low energy), you should "circle the wagons" and spend time studying from other outside sources. Artist often create amazing pieces when they have been inspired by others and so can the master sales person who is constantly looking for new ideas and inspiration.

*On the mid cycles spend your thought energy on staying completely engaged. Stay late and be involved as much as possible. These changing mini-sales seasons allow you to spend your time most effectively from cycle to cycle.

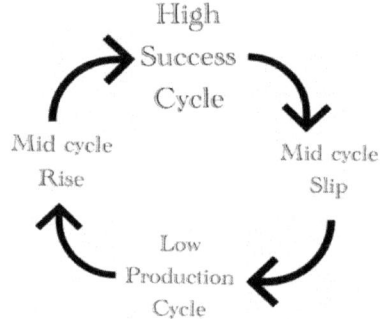

    Make a commitment to stay steady, energized and balanced in your pursuit of sales mastery. A long-distance runner competing in a marathon is focused on steady increase more than getting to the front of the pack immediately. Pepe Le Pu is a great example. His steady, constant and enthusiastic pursuit always seemed to work out and without over-exerted effort. Saving energy to be transmutated when the timing is right.

    You cannot allow yourself to get complacent. Instead choose to be a person of increase. Increase and growth are your goals because the universe we live in has cycles of life through an orchestrated rhythm. All things are in a state of growth or decay. Focusing your thought vibration energy and unwavering determination towards growth and increase, will keep you on the upward spiral of the sales cycle.

Knowing this law can give hope to any and all that embrace its natural beauty. Accept change is constant and make a commitment to stay rock steady through all conditions.

Think of good times when you're challenged and remember all the effort involved and all those that assisted when you're having great success. Balanced, focused and determined thought vibrations will be like an umbrella to all of life´s issues raining down upon you.

How can you become someone who is always increasing and growing?

What is the best way to stay steady as you pass through the sales cycles?

How is it possible to remain positive, no matter where you are currently in the sales cycle?

What is the most important action you can take to embrace the law of rhythm?

Do you already know what I am about to say? Service first frequency, protecting your thought vibrations, staying enthusiastic about your position and being grateful for each day and its inherent opportunities are key.

When you are in a service first frequency, you are not concerned about your recent performance, you're simply focused on your customer's needs. When you are protecting your thoughts, you don't allow negative people or negative talk to trans-mutate your energy from positive to negative. When you are staying enthusiastic, you are not distracted or spending up your thought vibration energy on worry or lack. When you are grateful for each day, you can separate results from your efforts and be happy driving home regardless if you've made a sale today or not.

Welcome to the new Master of the Sales Universe YOU... Solid, steady, happy, vibrant, enthusiastic, grateful and always with a service first thought vibration. Buy in and trust the process.

"Master stability with rhythm"

"Figure out the rhythm of life and live in harmony with it."; "Composure is the ruler of instability" Lao Tzu

"Walk with me and work with me – watch how I do it. Learn the unforced rhythms of grace." Matthew 11:29

5. THE LAW OF POLARITY

Everything that exists has a spectrum of extremes, or polar opposites

Many will tell you that the meaning of the Law of Polarity, is that everything has an opposite. However, this is not an accurate explanation of the law, in my humble opinion. When you dissect this very special law of the universe you will discover why it is such a valuable and significant piece to sales success. The Law of Polarity states that everything in existence has a spectrum of extremes, or polar opposites. Any example can apply:

Size extremes from **big** to, **small**.

Weather extremes from **hot** to, **cold.**

Wealth extremes from **rich** to, **poor**.

Hardness extremes from **indestructible** to, **soft**.

Frequency waves from **high** to, **low frequency**.

Take size as an example. Big is a size and small is a size, they are just opposite ends, of the same thing. Big cannot exist without small. There is no rich without poverty. You will learn in a future chapter that the Law of Relativity explains that the only way to relate something is to compare it with something else. Everything just is, until it is compared with something else. Extremes exist in every form. You can recognize the existence of both, by knowing that one cannot exist without the other. This even applies to situations in your sales meetings. *Situational extremes from positive to negative situations.*

Every situation arrives with **both positive and negative conditions**, simultaneously.

Ex: You are offered a great new sales position in a different city. The job comes with a 30% pay raise from your current position. However, you have had the same circle of friends for more than 10 years and the new job will require you to move away, start over and make new friends. The situation brings both positive and negative elements.

Breaking up with someone, after years of partnership, brings emotional pain and fear of the unknown. However, there is also the excitement of meeting someone new and what new experiences that will bring. Experiences that wouldn't have occurred, if not for the break up.

Applying the law of polarity to your sales career will revolutionize your mind-set and shift your thinking. How does knowing about the opposite ends of any spectrum, helpful to your sales career? How will mastering the law of polarity bring balance to your thought vibrations and your broadcast frequency? How will focusing your thought vibrations on the positive aspects of all situations affect your ability to magnetize what you want through the law of attraction? Can you recognize the value of knowing all the natural laws and how they work together?

What if you were able to realize that with all situations there will be positive and negative outcomes? What if you only focused your attention, efforts, action taking and thought vibrations on the positive? Where you focus your thought vibrations, is where your energy flows. When you focus on the positive potential and spend no time distracted with the negative, something profound can occur. You will always go into any situation knowing that positive elements exist. You will be able to find those positive elements and gain from all situations, no matter how perceived. You will also know, from this law, that no problem can exist without a solution. Note that it is much easier to determine what the positive or negative components are, in any situation, once you have identified your **core values**. Core values, should be written out and identified as soon as possible. ₈Lao Tzu explains that, "there are many paths to enlightenment. Be sure to take the one with a heart." What values are most important to you? What values are above all others in your sales career? How can the Law of Polarity be used to create sales success in your career?

YOU CAN LOOK FOR THE POSITIVE FACTORS IN ALL SITUATIONS BECAUSE THEY ARE THERE WAITING FOR YOU TO FIND THEM

Eureka! If you had not found a golden nugget yet in these pages, this must assuredly be one! Focus your attention on the positive side of the situational spectrum to get the best results!

For example, you take a written exam for a state license and somehow you don't pass the test by two answers. Now you must wait 45 days before taking the exam again.

What positive and negative elements can you take away from this example? How would you apply the law of polarity to this example? What positive elements would your thought vibrations focus on? How could this situation be turned into a positive?

You meet a person on the street. You know inherently, that this person will have positive and negative personality traits. You focus your attention on the positive qualities of that person. That person reciprocates the vibration back to you and matches your frequency.

You meet a new prospect. You know inherently, that your new prospect has positive and negative personality traits. You focus your attention and thought vibrations onto their positive personality traits. The prospect reciprocates your positive energy, enthusiasm and likes your service first vibration and begins to participate in the sales process.

Include in your sales goals how you will focus on the positive personality traits of your prospects each day. What kind of rapport and trust can you create with your prospect? How helpful will this connection be when you want to trans-mutate the sales seed energy? How helpful would it be to recognize the most positive elements to any and all of life's situations?

Mastering the law of polarity is like having a degree in optimism. Once the habit has taken shape, you will not look at any situation the same way again. No need to fret, all problems have a solution. You can now turn negative situations into positive repositions. You can now take a different approach to the world around you.

There cannot be wins without losses and when you choose to seek out the positives from each situation you can take positives from all wins and losses. This means that even when you lose, if you are able to trans-mutate the most positive elements from that situation and you increase and grow regardless. Maintaining the upward sales cycle even when you fail short of a commitment to purchase.

When you are in your next **_low production cycle_** in your sales career, choose to spend time focused on the positive. You've identified that your situation has a solution. You begin working on your sales presentation to create something more effective. You keep your thought vibrations focused on positive inspirational messaging. You find inspiration, it changes your vibrational energy. You now have an inspired idea or technique, that you would have never developed if it had not been for the sales slump. Thus, turning a negative situation into a positive solution.

Now you can convert a negative to a positive by simply applying the law of polarity. By focusing your thought vibrations on solution-based positive imagery. Now you can convert any obstacle into discoverable solution.

You can turn complacency into inspiration like a Judo or Aikido master, using your opponent's momentum into your momentum. Only in sales there is no enemy except the space between your ears. Your customer is not your enemy or opponent. Your customer's reasons not to buy your product can become the reasons they do buy, when the law of Polarity is understood and applied to your life and sales career.

Example: we are not going to buy your product right now because we really haven't taken many vacations over the last few years

Response: It's exactly the reason you should be buying, so you can always plan to spend time together and be committed. Most of our members have purchased because they want to go on more vacations. You are likely not to change your habits unless you have a plan that will help you.

How would you feel about having a plan in place to make sure you always can go and stay somewhere amazing on vacation? Having a plan would actually help encourage your family to go more often, wouldn't it?

Keep your thought vibrations focused on gratitude and look for the positive in everything because it is there. The reason you want to keep your focus on gratitude is to keep your vibrational energy from reaching emotional extremes. Your emotional state has polar extremes too, and in order to be a Master of the Sales Universe you will want to balance those extremes with a calmness that comes from knowing that every situation contains positive elements which can be embraced and wielded for your use.

"Master positive perspective"

"New beginnings are often disguised as painful endings" Lao Tzu

"Man is made or unmade by himself; in the armoury of thought he forges the weapons by which he destroys himself; he also fashions the tools with which he builds for himself heavenly mansions of joy and strength and peace. By the right choice and true application of thought, man ascends to the Divine Perfection; by the abuse and wrong application of thought, he descends below the level of the beast. Between these two extremes are all the grades of character, and man is their maker and master." James Allen

6. THE LAW OF GESTATION

Everything manifests after an incubation process

The Law of Gestation explains that there is a process of growth with all things in order for them to exist. Place a seed in the soil, make sure the seeded area gets plenty of sunlight and water. The seed will open beneath the soil and sprout toward the surface and sunlight. In time, the sprout matures and becomes a plant. The plant does not just instantly appear because it must grow through a process. If you are a mother, you know how long 9 months of pregnancy can be (actually fathers know too) because babies don't just appear. It takes time for the baby to grow in the womb before its developed enough to live independently. Everything, in fact, that exists in the world began as a seed and manifests into its intended self through an initial growth process and sustained energy.

Sequoia trees are the best example, in the plant kingdom, of how something so meniscal can grow into the largest living organism in the world. If you ever have the opportunity to go to the Sequoia Park in California and step into the visitor's center, there are examples of the Sequoia tree seeds. The seeds are so small that it takes [9]125,000 seeds to weigh 1 pound. From this tiny seed grows the largest living organism on Earth. The largest Sequoia tree, the General Sherman, weighs 2.7 million pounds and stands at 275 feet in height and is incredibly impressive in person. I have stood in front of General Sherman on several occasions and I always think of the incredible design of creation and how the law of gestation can, in time, create the most amazing things imaginable.

In 2010, the United States was recovering from a massive real estate collapse and many real estate projects through-out North America were failing. These effects carried over into developments in Mexico resort areas. Business was down everywhere.

In the same year one of my mentors, Terry Harker and his wife Jenny, were flying on a plane from British Columbia, Canada back to Cabo San Lucas, Mexico. Terry had worked for many years as a sales director in timeshare and had recently retired. Terry had changed his appearance by growing a thick and unkept beard (a symbol of his unemployed freedom) and did not look like someone who was about to hatch a multi-million-dollar idea, while flying to the Mexican beach paradise. Terry, in mid-flight, had a flash of genius. He envisioned a timeshare project that would include a golf course as the centerpiece. He started jotting down his ideas on an airplane napkin. The notes on the napkin were like a Sequoia seed just waiting to be planted in fertile soil.

    After landing in Cabo San Lucas, Terry reached out to his friend and former associate, Brent Underdahl. Brent and Terry met up and decided to pursue the idea, using their own money to create a sales and marketing company. Next, they began to approach real estate projects in Los Cabos, looking for a business partner with a golf course to follow their dream. Upon their search, they found a fifteen-hundred-acre waterfront community, named Diamante, that had soft opened in 2008, right before the real estate market collapse. Though the property had minimal infrastructure in place, it was also spectacular. Diamante Cabo San Lucas had been a Lehman Brothers project, but after the U.S. real estate market collapse, Ken Jowdy the developer of Diamante, was doing his best to weather the storm and maintain his vision for the project, despite the most challenging external conditions. Terry and Brent tried to set up a meeting with Mr. Jowdy to present their concept of fractionally sold properties on the Diamante development. Ken refused to meet with them. Terry and Brent came to the golf clubhouse daily to eat breakfast. The story goes that after 30 days of consistently showing up to the property, Ken finally decided to meet with them. Ken explained his vision, Brent and

Terry took that vision and created a product that would fit his vision. From there the small sales company was formed called 'Ironman Marketing' (from their years of competing in Ironman competitions together). Nine years later and the Diamante is an extremely successful development in Mexico, featuring a Davis Love & Tiger Woods golf course, a 10-acre Crystal Lagoon pool, and new Nobu and Hard Rock Hotel on the beach front.

Follow the **gestation** period, from Terry's **idea** (*thought vibration &* seed) written on a napkin, then **energy** (*efforts and actions taken*) applied and **unwavering persistence** (*they came every day until he would meet with them*). The result was a multi-million-dollar company and the creation of one of the best private golf communities in North America.

There are countless examples of this process. Johnny Morris, started the [10]Bass Pro Shop stores selling bait from an 8-square-foot of space in the back of his father's liquor store. Today the Bass Pro Shop concept has 200 retail stores and Johnny Morris is worth 6.8 billion dollars (Forbes).

I write about the Diamante, in particular, because I lived it. I made a vision board in 2010 and had decided I wanted to work at a development that included world class golf. The seed for my next sales adventure was planted. A few months later the softball season began and Terry and I were playing on the same team. I learned about Terry and Brent's project before anyone (law of attraction through the law of vibration) and decided to go see it (looked like my vision board). I remember coming home the day I first saw the development and telling my kids, "Daddy found the promised land". In 2011, Ironman's first year open, I sold 3.4 million dollars of fractional properties and an additional 3.5 million in traditional real estate. I was awarded the sales person of the year and enjoyed an all- expense paid trip to the Super Bowl (in Indy) with Terry and Brent, which we arrived to the stadium in a white limo and in full referee outfits. You can also create exciting results in your life and career by being specific with what you want and holding that energy as your seed. Here's the formula:

Seed planted + nurtured action + incubation = existence

Thought vibrational frequency + energy + persistence = manifestation

Apply this cycle to anything you want in your career. For example, you are selling the same amount of watches every month and you want to double your production.

What is the seed you want to plant into your mental garden?

<u>You want to double your production (so be specific)</u>

What types of actions will you take to nurture your seed?

<u>You will learn how to close more frequently or learn to upsell your customer</u>

How should you apply your energy to help the seed grow?

<u>EX: instead of watching tv every day you view videos on sales techniques and create your own style and approach</u>

How will you apply unwavering persistence to grow your seed into something BIG?

<u>The choices you make will reflect the amount of persistence you are applying because unwavering means there is no flexibility in your commitment</u>

Will you follow through until it happens?

Not getting frustrated if the first new technique you create does not produce the desired result, continue the pursuit with a clear vision of the end result

When you were born, people began to see the traits of your parents in you. *The seed you plant will resemble the culmination of your thought vibrations.* If your vision is blurry, so shall the result. *Best to be very clear.* If the soil you are planting your seed is toxic, the seed will not survive. *Best to not hold grudges, forgive people quickly to not harbor negative energy (as you learned in the chapter on the law of Trans-mutation). Best to not be around negative people who will lower your vibrational frequency to fear or doubt.*

The traits and characteristics of your seed will come from your very own thought vibrations and they will attract like energies and trans-mutate into their vision form. Knowing that there is a time period before that new form takes shape allows you to be patient and persistent, trusting the process.

Being persistent in the pursuance of your vision is an upward spiral of growth. Growth is learning. Growth is making painful mistakes, but not making them again. Growth is perpetual. Growth is the natural way. Many elements can stun growth and that it why it is so important to create an environment of constant growth and not to get frustrated when the results you want haven't instantly appeared. When you understand this law enough to mastery, you can procure the natural cycle and enjoy each part of the growth process. 25**James Allen** expressed it well when he wrote, "*Just as a gardener cultivates his plot, keeping it free from weeds, and growing the flowers and fruits which he requires, so may a man tend the garden of his mind, weeding out all the wrong, useless, and impure thoughts, and cultivating toward perfection the flowers and fruits of right, useful, and pure thoughts. By pursuing this process, a man sooner or later discovers that he is the master-gardener of his soul, the director of his life. He also reveals, within himself, the laws of thought, and understands, with ever-increasing accuracy, how the thought-forces and mind elements operate in the shaping of his character, circumstances, and destiny.*"

Every idea you have is like a seed. Your choice to plant the seed and to nurture it requires energy. If you plant your seed in a mind of doubt and non-belief, what do you suppose will happen to that seed? If you have a great idea for a new style of lounge chair, will it just suddenly appear? What would you need to do in order to take a great idea and turn it into an actual chair or even a business venture? Can you see that everything that exist requires time to manifest? What would you consider are the most important concepts that you can take away from the law of gestation?

[8]Lao Tzu wrote, "Be careful what you water your dreams with. Water them with worry and fear and you will produce weeds that choke the life from your dream. Water them with optimism and solutions and you will cultivate success. Always be on the lookout for ways to turn a problem into an opportunity for success. Always be on the lookout for ways to nurture your dreams."

Imagine you create a vision of something that you want in your sales career. If you truly stay focused on accomplishing your goals and you know that they will manifest, as long as you are applying energy (thought vibrations) and unwavering commitment, once the incubation process is complete. This is the reason I prefer to use the garden and seed reference because its inherent in nature and an example that anyone can follow.

[11]**Gandhi** once said, "to forget how to dig the earth and tend the soil is to forget ourselves". If you do not tend to your mind's soil it will be difficult to grow anything with your seeds because they will wither in the incubation

process. Your seeds will need to be planted in fertile soil. Fertile soil, in this case, being a mental garden without toxic elements which kill the seeds before they can grow. Fear, regret, doubt, resentment and many other negative thought vibrations can completely sabotage your garden's success. This also applies to your customer's mind garden, which you will want to manage well to keep their objectivity fertile. Finding out your customer's opinion on your product or your industry, for example, can lead to pulling out the weeds that won't let your sales seed grow otherwise. Because if you don't find out that the prospect's brother bought some similar product to the one you are selling and his brother hates it, you won't know that there are weeds in the garden that you will need to remove before you plant your sale seeds. Without a proper discovery process in the beginning of your sales meeting you will not make sales AND you won't know why either, so remove the weeds before planting your sales seeds. Make sense?

    Every idea you have is like a seed. Plant too many seeds, it might be difficult to apply enough energy to grow them all at once. If you don't plant enough seeds and you won't have anything growing. We can plant seeds into our customer's thought vibrations and with proper nurturing it will grow into a sale, but you need to know what your customer wants to grow. If your customer is not motivated by status, don't spend time telling your customer that your product will make them look good in the eyes of others. If your customer wants to impress a woman with an engagement ring, then you will plant a seed like "the ring you choose will be the everlasting symbol of your love and commitment to her, which ring in this display do you think says that best?" Is your **sales seed compelling** and powerful enough to be remembered for years to come? What questions and power statements can you use, during your prospect's gestation period, to create more sales success? Is it wise to write down a list of questions you can ask to best understand your customer's vision? How many **power statements** can you create that are relevant to your product? How can you use those **power statements** to pour miracle grow on your seeded soil? Are you using **feature, benefit, tie down commitments** to create a bond with your customer and your product?

- This feature is something that you told me you like, the benefit to you would be x, y and z, this will be fantastic to have in your life, wouldn't you agree? Confirm that your customer would like having that feature because of the benefits to them.

That makes sense, doesn't it? You'd probably wear this jacket almost every day, wouldn't you? You like where this book is going, don't you? It seems to be way better than what you have been doing, don't you agree?

Here's a sales analogy I used to hear often:

Imagine the sales process is a semi-truck with trailer, and your customer is the precious cargo on the trailer. You will want to stop, get out and tie down your cargo a few times along the way, otherwise, you run the risk of your cargo falling off before you get there.

Apply the law of gestation to your sales process and understand that you don't want the energy to subside while the gestation timing takes shape. Remember that, unlike a baby or plant, there is no set time for a sale to gestate. Each customer will vary in that regard. Your main focus can be to stay engaged, without distraction, and focus your thought vibrations on a service first frequency broadcast. It's a warm vibrational energy like a heating lamp over eggs in a hatchery. Being grateful that if for some reason, this sales seed doesn't grow in your prospect's soil, <u>you will grow</u> regardless from the experience and be prepared better for the next prospect. This gratitude and vibrational frequency, will be how you manage yourself through the gestation period of your next big career seed that you have planted and are nurturing into existence. Mastering the law of Gestation allows you to have perspective over results and patience while manifesting your vision into existence.

You can apply the law of gestation to this very book you are reading. I have been a top performer and sales trainer for more than two decades, but this book could not have been written 20 years ago because it's taken, a twenty-year sales career with hundreds of books consumed and thousands of happy customers to gestate the seed of this book into existence. Though it's taken much time to manifest, it's timing could not be more suitable because the beauty of any piece of work is derived from the consideration and effort involved.

"Master to trust in the process"

"An awakened imagination works with a purpose. It creates and conserves the desirable, and transforms and destroys the undesirable" Neville Goddard

"Adopt the pace of nature: her secret is patience" Ralph Waldo Emerson

7. THE LAW OF RELATIVITY

Everything just IS, until it is compared to something else

The law of relativity is an amazing reminder that the only way to have perspective of something, is to compare it with something else. Everything relates to everything else and everything is relative. How can we know what tall is unless we have something short to compare it with? Perspective of the perceived "something" is relative to your mindset. Everything is relative by a standard of comparison and is normally visually observable.

There are noticeable characteristics, in each individual item that exists, that allow it to be compared to other items through observation and a process of dissemination.

Each of us, as human beings, are completely autonomous and have our own paths to take in our lives and sales careers. Because of your nature to understand and compare, in order to differentiate yourself from others, you should remain deliberate and diligent to the inherent pitfalls that come with comparing yourself to someone else. Comparing yourself with others can be done on different levels of comparison. You can be jealous of other's successes without knowing all the relevant information necessary to truly understand their situation. Comparing your weaknesses to someone else's strengths can lead to a negative emotional energy, which is the anthesis of faith. Allowing 'your perspective' to work against your own better interests. The [8]**Tao Te Ching** explains that, "*When you are content to be simply yourself and don't compare or compete, everyone will respect you.*" You will learn in this chapter that you can relatively compare yourself to others, all while appreciating that every person has a different path to take and that you should not compare yourself to others based on external elements alone because it is not possible to know all variables involved.

    The Law of Relativity should be mastered by all those who are looking to create increase in their lives and careers. If you are seeking higher levels of achievement, you will want to release the deep feelings of inadequacy that can develop internally when you don't apply the law to your advantage. Some have labeled this law, the law of comparison. When you recognize this law's existence, it can empower and embolden you. If you choose to ignore or not develop an understanding of the law, it can destroy you from within through self-ridicule or judgment. Imagine being trapped in a cycle of comparisons, where you can ONLY be satisfied if you achieve EQUAL TO OR BEYOND the perceived comparative variable (co-worker, college friend, family member, etc.). Meaning that your career happiness is based on comparing your production to someone else's production. This could lead you into a dark place of regret and shame or a total lack of appreciation for your unique talents and situation. However, when you use the **law of comparison** with a **lens of gratitude**, the law can become a great guide to your personal development.

In the bible it says in Matthew 12:37, "For by your words you will be justified, and by your words you will be condemned". Your words and your thoughts are things, they are energy. If you are comparing yourself to someone else you should make sure you are applying the correct lens to use. How do you apply relative perspective to your advantage? It can be done with protected thought vibrations during the perspective process. Like a filter or lens, you will consider your current sales career position as a relative position.

One of my former sales managers, Chris Ross, often said, "perception is reality" and he was most definitely correct. Perception is what you use when you analyze and compare. I believe that it is **HOW we compare things** (in what lens are you looking at this through) that makes the difference in what and how you manifest. When you consider that in your life you will encounter people who you may perceive to be in a better situation than you. You may perceive that they (comparative variable) have been more successful than you or that they have more natural beauty than you see in yourself. For example, what would you perceive about a couple flying on their private jet for a vacation to Mauritius? Would you perceive them to be in a better situation than you? There are also people you perceive to be in a better situation than theirs. For example, the guy in dirty clothes asking for change when you leave the convenience store. So, on a scale of comparison you can deduct there are people both in a better and or worse situation than you, meaning that your situation is relative to everyone else.

In [12]*A New Earth: Awakening Your Life's Purpose*, **Eckhart Tolle** says, *"In form, you are and will always be inferior to some, superior to others. In essence, you are neither inferior nor superior to anyone. True self-esteem and true humility arise out of that realization. In the eyes of the ego, self-esteem and humility are contradictory. In truth, they are one and the same."* This is a fabulous observation and reveals much about the relativeness of perspective and that self-esteem and humility are components of mental balance, and not contradictory as some may perceive. This means that it is possible to have a high self-esteem AND be humble when dealing with others. Humility lessens the focus on self-absorption and yet can also boost your self-esteem by reinforcing your balanced mental concept of relativity. If you are, as Tolle says, "neither inferior or superior to anyone", then you are free from the law of comparison's grip on your psyche and you can now move on with your career in a new and broadened perspective state.

The great Roman Emperor Marcus Aurelius had much to say on this subject, as it is a theme spread throughout his writings. [13]Mediations, is a collection of Aurelius' personal journals. Through his observations, Marcus Aurelius suggests to step out of your peripheral perspective by visualizing a perspective above yourself. Providing insight into the conditions outside of your limited perspective. It could be compared to seeing your life from a video game perspective. There is now overwhelming evidence that using this OUTSIDE or second person perspective can have great effects on energy and performance.

A Banglor University study from [14]July 10, 2019 revealed that athletes using the self-talk encouragement in the *second person* pronoun performed at a higher level than athletes using self-talk in the *first-person* pronoun. This evidence gives credence to Marcus Aurelius' outer perspective vantage point. The study found that, "*There are of course different types of tasks associated with sports and much less is known about endurance tasks which is why we applied this to cycling.*" "*Our findings from 16 active males indicate that second person self-talk generated significantly greater power output and faster time-trial performance than first person self-talk. Interestingly, the participants did not report noticing any difference in ratings of perceived exertion. So, they were able to do more work but didn't notice any difference in workload.*" Upon researching this subject further, I discovered there were many such articles, all over the internet, exploring that second person (outer perspective) self-talk is more effective than using first person. What would be a reason that second person self-talk is more effective than first person?

Are you using self-talk in your daily preparation or during the sales process with your prospect? Could it give you an advantage, to self-talk in the second person? How could you gain from looking at your life from a higher or outer perspective than you are doing now?

"Everything we hear is an opinion, not a fact. Everything we see is a perspective, not the truth"

"You have a power over your mind – not outside events. Realize this, and you will find strength"

13 Marcus Aurelius

Often, you won't know enough about someone's situation to make an assessment in the first place. It is easy to make quick judgments about your sales prospect and, as you now know, those judgments may be affected by your mental state and your thought vibrations. If you are worried about a personal situation back at home and your thought vibrations are not focused on your sales presentation then it is also likely to affect how you perceive your customer?

- Does this person look like they're going to buy something?
- These people are like the rude couple from last week, I'll get through this quick.
- People from _____ never buy anything.

Perspective is relative to how we perceive our customers. Protecting your thoughts, staying in a high vibrational frequency and increasing your state of humility will decrease the 'judgments' you make about your prospects. When you have mastered the law of relativity you will no longer judge any prospect you meet or you if you do you will quickly shift your judgement, once you've reminded yourself of these teachings and you again are reminded that **every person is constantly buying things they need**, and so everyone, for that reason, is a prospect and a potential customer. That is how repeat customers are nurtured into lifetime customers. You can use the law of comparison as a balancing act and as a reminder to never prejudge any prospect. A customer is relative to your thought vibrational frequency.

Remember:

- **All prospects are relative, meaning they are neither good nor bad.**
- **All prejudgments made of prospects are based on your vibrational frequency and deductions from perspective.**
- **All prospects should be treated as individuals standing alone and without comparison.**
- **All prospects should experience the entire sales process to prevent prejudging from deductions made from perspective.**
(remember trust in the process)

Perspective, therefore, can only provide a limited amount of truth regarding any situation. For example, there have been people caught begging for money from people on the streets, only to be filmed, followed and discovered to be charlatans. People pretending to be needy homeless people to deceive good Samaritans. There are people who seem to have nice material things, but have no savings and are pretending to be wealthier than they actually are. On the contrary, many of the wealthiest people in the world dress down to the perception of what someone with wealth would dress like (even that is relative). Our perceptions can often be inaccurate because a lack of knowledge (lack of correct information).

Due to perception being a reality (in your mind), I recommend that you **stay away from comparing yourself** to others. **Make it a habit. Consider your sales career much like a professional golfer.** A pro golfer will have a coach or coaches to get expert advice. A pro golfer does compete with other pro golfers, but indirectly. Each golfer keeps their own score and is focused on their shot by shot performance. If at the end of the round, their score is best they will receive their desired reward. A pro golfer cannot be concerned about what the rest of the field is doing or they risk the mental distraction that comes from splitting their mind from the task at hand to pre occupation with the competitors. Do you think Tiger Woods is focusing his thought vibrations on the other competitors or is he completely focused on his game and efforts?

Remember that no matter your current situation there are many others in a worse situation than you. Find gratitude to be in your situation and consider it to be your path on the way to achievement.

To be a Master of the Sales Universe, you should perceive yourself relative to your sales career. There will be salespeople ahead of you in the field and there will be those that don't make the cut and your only focus will be growth and achievement using your new lens of relativity through gratitude.

"Master humility and self-esteem through a relative perception"

"Acknowledging the good that you already have in your life is the foundation for all abundance" Eckhart Tolle

"Believe in yourself and don't try to convince others. Be content without yourself, and don't need other's approval. Accept who you

are, and the whole world will accept you."
Tao Te Ching - Stanza 30

8. THE LAW OF CAUSE AND EFFECT

For every action there is an equal and opposite reaction

"**Every why hath a wherefore**"

William Shakespeare

Shakespeare, DaVinci, Plato, Emerson, and many great influential thinkers have all concluded that everything that exists and the way it exists, has an origin. The Law of Cause and Effect is the explanation for the origin of all things. This encompassing law concludes that there is no effect without a cause or as the Roman philosopher [15]**Lucretius** once wrote, "*nothing comes from nothing*". Whatever it may be, there was a cause to create it. Try to think of something, anything, that doesn't have a cause. I won't wait for your answer because the only explanation to anything's existence is cause and effect. This universal law will bring you joy on many levels because when you discover that a certain cause will have a certain effect you can choose to emulate those causes to have a positive and similar effect on your life.

Consistently think and act on your vision to be effective at getting it because every

thought and action you take will have effect on your process.

For example, if you choose to look for something each day to be grateful for, the effect would be that you would be more in tune to all the goodness in your life. If you choose to focus on something each day you want to improve a little bit, how refined will that skill set be in one month? How about a year from now? Would the cause of daily self-improvement effect your performance at work? (ode to rhetorical questions)

What effects do you desire to enjoy in your life? What daily causes can be done to be ever increasingly closer to your desired effect? Sometimes, if you work backwards and reverse engineer your goals, the path to get there becomes much clearer.

If someone is over-weight or in perfect physical condition, there is a cause for that effect. If you spent 1 extra hour per day working on improving your sales skill sets, how long would it take to have a great effect on your production? What if you never made time to work on your sales skills, could you still expect to have great results? What if you analyze the effect that you want first and then determine what types of causes will need to occur for you to experience that effect.

- I want to be this ***person*** _____
- What actions will I take to become that ***person***?
- What types of habits does that ***person*** have?
- Who am I now?
- How far am I from being that ***person***?
- What will I do each day to become that ***person***?

Consistency in thought can be the cause of amazing effects, no different than the dripping of water on to a stone tablet. Eventually the water will make a hole through the stone by persistence over time. Cause and effect.

Here is a great exercise to begin developing this habit. First of all, buy a journal to take notes and create your exact description of ***who that person is you are evolving into***. Something I learned from Chris Shryack at Performance with Power, is an exercise designed to create positive movement in all facets of your life. The exercise is simple, but challenging too if you are fully applying yourself. Write down:

I AM _____

(characteristics of the desired person effects)

I recommend you spend some time and write down as many as you can think of. ***I am kind. I am always growing. I am immune to ridicule. I am better than yesterday.*** Who are you becoming? What types of habits does that person you are becoming, embrace to reach their goals? What type of habits do successful people proactively implement to reach similar goals? Do you think if you had similar habits to those of highly effective sales people in your industry that you too would have similar results? What if you knew about habits that people use to create high levels of success, but you decide not to adapt those habits into your life, what will the results be? In my mind, this is the beauty of the law of cause and effect because you don't have to reinvent the wheel again to create results in your sales career. Other fantastic sales people and leaders of industry have already created many wonderful success recipes to follow. Additionally, there are many great sales gurus on the internet with an abundance of closing techniques and styles of approach that can be learned and adapted into your life and habits.

Take the law of reciprocation as an example of the cause and effect phenomena. First, find something that you genuinely like about your customer. This will cause your customer to return the affection because it is our nature to like those who like us, when it is expressed genuinely (high vibrational frequency). This Cause, no matter how underlying, will have a great effect on your client. This can only be accomplished with your inner love reflecting your exterior world and your customer feeling that vibrational energy. Inner health and humility reflect outer health and kindness. Giving love to your customer will result in a reflection of that love returned (every action has an equal or opposite reaction) and the best part is that no matter the final outcome, all parties leave the sales experience with a high vibrational frequency and mutually endearing sentiments. Obviously, you always want to close the sale, but this **love vibration** practiced daily will have profound and compounding effects. It will keep your energy positive and prevent you from getting sour grapes with non-buyers. Charismatic, humorous, genuine and grounded will be how your customers would describe you because you have balanced your mental awareness between high self-esteem and humility. In fact, the more you do to guide your thought vibrations to a relative place of possibility and ever increase, the greater effect it will have on your daily results. The increased results will perpetuate into a lifetime habit because the cause has proven the effect.

Follow proven success methods then use your imagination and unique perspective to adopt that method into your vibrational frequency energy. Make it your own method.

Find out what the most successful people are doing, in your industry, and follow those same methods to get similar results, but I cannot impress upon you enough to adjust the method *into your method*. Own it. Repeating exactly what someone else says does not necessarily create the same results because, as you might remember from a previous chapter, words only make up 8% of the approximate communication, so repeating someone's words will not be extremely effective. However, if you make the message '*your message*' and deliver it in a way that '*only you can*', then the same words can become very powerful due to the vibrational energy attached to the message.

Taking responsibility for the effects in your life and in your career, is vital to your power and confidence because once you have taken full responsibility for every effect that has occurred in your life, you will have reached a new level of self-awareness. Your will power and confidence will also reach new heights because you no longer give the excuses any power. When you blame someone else for the results (effects) in your life you are relinquishing your own energy and vibrational power. Lower power equals lower frequency.

[16]**Jimi Kwik** has a great analogy regarding taking responsibility for the effects in your life. He says, "*You can be a thermostat or you can be a thermometer. One sets the environment the other reacts to the environment.*" This is an exceptional analogy of how being pro-active puts you ahead of the cause and effect curve and can help you make large shifts in your sales success.

"Master creating better effects through proactive causes"

"Nature is the source of all true knowledge. She has her own logic her own laws and she has no effect without cause nor invention without necessity" Leonardo DaVinci

"Nothing comes from nothing" Lucretius

"Cause and effect is the law of laws" Ralph Waldo Emerson

**"Only by much searching and mining, are gold and diamonds obtained, and man can find every truth connected with his being, if he will dig deep into the mine of his soul; and that he is the maker of his character, the moulder of his life, and the builder of his destiny, he may unerringly prove, if he will watch, control, and alter his thoughts, tracing their effects upon himself, upon others, and upon his life and circumstances, linking cause and effect by patient practice and investigation, and utilizing his every experience, even to the most trivial, everyday occurrence, as a means of obtaining that knowledge of himself which is Understanding, Wisdom, Power. In this direction, as in no other, is the law absolute that "He that seeketh findeth; and to him that knocketh it shall be opened; for only by patience, practice, and ceaseless importunity can a man enter the Door of the Temple of Knowledge." [25]James Allen

9. THE LAW OF GENDER

Everything has masculine and feminine components

There are two powerful forces that create balance in the universe; masculine and feminine. These forces mold mind, body and soul into form. Creation cannot exist without both forces coming together. The law of gestation could not exist without a female and male component. Lack of femininity, allows the masculine force to lead without restraint and contrarily lack of masculinity results in stagnation and lack of action.

When both Masculine and Feminine forces are working together, there is a synergy that results in creation, at which point both the Feminine and the Masculine fulfill which the other lacks to make whole. Both forces merge and from it we become a part of each. In other words, you have both masculine and feminine traits as a human being. For the purpose of this book, you will look into the contrasts of gender and how to create your sales persona through incorporating both masculine and feminine energies into sales tools which can be applied daily.

The Yin and Yang symbol, or Tàijítu, is often associated with the masculine and feminine relationship of coexistence. Day turns to night and night turns into day and the balance that each brings to the other exemplifies the complimentary nature of the law. There is femininity in the masculine and there is masculine in femininity and each thrives from the others existence. Natural beauty related through balance. In the book, THE LIGHT WILL SET YOU FREE, [17]**Milanovich** and **McCuny** write, *"We must learn to balance the yin and yang in our thoughts, emotions, words and actions to a point of stability (androgyny) or mental balance, so that we'll intuitively know how and when to act in alignment with our "androgynous" Higher Self".*

I believe there is a sales lesson that lies beneath the surface of this law and once you've mastered it, you will be more balanced and adept to take on any sales situation from a balanced position.

In absence of the masculine element there is an absence of stability and confidence. I find this to be incontrovertible when you look at the tons of research on the subject of children growing up without a father figure (masculine influence).

In 2007 [18]**Sarah Allen**, MSc and **Kerry Daly**, PhD (University of Gulph) from Ontario, Canada wrote a paper on masculine influence with child development with a massive amount of supporting data. *Effects of the Father Involvement: A Summary of the Research Evidence.* The conclusions are astounding.

Children with **involved fathers** are more likely to ***demonstrate cognitive competence on standard intellectual assessments***, are more likely to ***enjoy school and participate in extracurricular activities***, are more likely to ***become educationally mobile and with higher levels of economic, educational and career successes***, are more likely to be ***socially mature and morally secure***, are more likely to be ***tolerant and socially understanding***, are ***less likely to be delinquents, drug users, truants or thieves***.

The variable that is most consistently associated with positive life outcomes is the quality of the father child relationship (**Amato**, 1988; **Furstenberg&Harris**, 1993; **Lamb**, 1997)

Children **without a father involved** in their lives are more likely to **have problems in school performance**; are more likely to **experience bad behavior problems at school**; are more likely to **have a lowered**

moral code and less likely to accept blame for transgressions; are more likely to **cheat and lie**; are more likely **to have emotional and psychological problems**; are more likely to **choose deviant peers as friends**; are more likely to **experience physical or emotional abuse**; are more likely to **engage in criminal behavior**; are more likely to **abuse illegal drugs or alcohol**.

Overall, men, who have involved fathers during early adulthood usually turn out to be good spouses, workers and citizens at midlife (**Snarey**, 1993)

I invite you the look up **Allen & Daly's** 2007 research to see the vast amount data that has gone into the making of their report. The evidence is clear that childhood development requires a masculine component in order to have a stable foundation and functioning moral compass.

Second, let's look at the effects of the feminine components and how they relate to development. What is more feminine than motherly love? Many scholars have detailed the effects of the feminine energy that is required in development. One expert, [19]**Erica Komisar**, a parenting advisor and psychoanalyst says from her research that, "A ***mother's physical and emotional presence provides*** babies with two things: ***protection from stress and emotional regulation***, both of which are important to healthy brain development and the ***child's future well-being***." "*If our mother isn't there to protect us from that stress that we feel, then it doesn't lay the foundation down to be resilient to stress in the future.*" Meaning, that during the first stages of development, it is required for the infant to experience the nurturing effects of the feminine components and without their existence the child grows up without the feeling of belonging and an absence of love vibration. Komisar says a hormone named oxytocin is released from the body when mothers and fathers nurture a child together. "*This is what we call 'the bonding hormone' or 'the love hormone.' The oxytocin mothers produce during bonding makes them more sensitive and empathic nurturers. Whereas the oxytocin that fathers produce in the same circumstance makes them more playfully stimulating and 'encouraging of children to be independent and explore.'*"

You can conclude from these findings that development of a human being, or the development of anything in creation requires a masculine and a feminine component to be balanced and complete. What about the development of a **sales seed**? Does your **sales seed** need a masculine and feminine component to have balance when creating your next sale? The answer is YES and here are some of the reasons why:

• Men and women buy for different reasons. To break it down to a simplistic explanation, men buy predominately on logic and women buy predominately on emotion. When you are selling to a couple, you will want to have a balance of logic and emotion infused into your selling points in order to appeal to both parties.

• Selling on logic alone will not help you hold a high closing percentage. Your product may make sense for them to own, but they are not feeling secure about moving forward or you have not created enough urgency for them to take action. Your sales seeds did not grow because you didn't make them feel the emotion to experience your product. This is a lack of the feminine component and you will want to have more emotional content, like painting a picture with your customers enjoying your product or using **third party selling stories**. You are not telling your customers what to do, but you are using examples of other people, much like themselves, who have had success with your product or people who have avoided painful situations because they have your product. Converting logic into an emotional story with balance.

• Selling on emotion alone will only get your customer into a different state (vibrational frequency). However, without having a logical reason to proceed with the purchase your customer will be excited until they realize it's not the right time to move forward. You need to present your product in such a way that you are helping them address a need that should be attended to immediately and the timing couldn't be better than right now. You will want to have the masculine components to balance the feminine emotions.

• Balance of engagement time with your customers (married couples) is very relevant. If you are engaged in conversation almost exclusively with the husband and ignore the required time to spend appealing to the wife, she will undoubtedly kill the sale upon the close. If you spent most of your time speaking to the wife, it is unlikely the husband is not paying attention to every word you say because most men will not have someone speaking to their wives without hearing everything going on in the conversation. I would recommend you focus more on the wife than the husband. In fact, if she gets emotional about your product, she is likely to do the heavy lifting and assist you with making the sale.

- Women, in general, do not like an aggressive or hard sale approach. You will want to spend time developing your skill sets for female customers. Women like to be noticed for their choices; like hair style, jewelry, clothing, etc., so include a genuine compliment about an article that you particularly like and comment about it. Women enjoy talking about their families and their children, so make sure to include in your warm up conversation some **open-ended questions** to allow them to open up about their children and in doing so will change their vibrational frequency to a heightened and favorable one. Also, all factors such as verbiage, tone of voice and body language will need to be masterfully woven through a series of conversational questions to maximize your success rate with your female customers. I recommend you practice your choice of words and tonality with a female friend or family member until you have a soft and natural delivery, like two friends in a hair salon catching up on what's new.

- Men, in general, like to be recognized for their qualities or accomplishments. Learning early about what a man does for a living and putting him on a pedestal of admiration (love vibration-genuine) will result in a responsive and active participant. This works because you are appealing to his masculine qualities as a provider and producer and he will reciprocate with eager participation.

The disclaimer to these following examples is that there are some women with an overdeveloped masculinity as well as some men whom have an overdeveloped femininity. In either case, you will need to make your best assessment on which approach you may choose to employ with them. This is another good reason to have a blend of both masculine and feminine energies when you are making your sales presentation.

Part of the technique can be speeding up and slowing down speech, depending upon what or whom you are appealing to during that particular juncture in your sales approach. You can also move in and out of dominate and subversive tonality, where your customer feels the frequencies of confidence combined with empathy.

Longtime FBI negotiator, turned business coach and author, [20]**Chris Voss**, addresses how to have *tactical empathy*, in his book *Never Split the Difference*. In the book he lists 3 voice tones available to negotiators which are; *the late-night FM DJ voice* (low, calming and trustworthy), *the positive/playful voice* (relax and smile while talking to create good-naturedness), *the direct or assertive voice* (to be used sparingly because of its aggressive nature). The nature behind these tone of voice techniques lies within the masculine and feminine domains. These, and other tone of voice options can either relieve stress and regulate emotion (feminine) or create foundation and trust (masculinity) on the basis of vibrational broadcast frequency. I encourage you to play around with your tonality to find your best tone of voice to create your desired results. You may want to record your voice while making your presentations to hear what your tonality sounds like and be prepared to cringe for the first few weeks, but the effort will be worth it when the results start to pile up.

One of my son's favorite internet memes is a photo of an enormous book with thousands of pages entitled "The Book of Understanding Women". The reason that even a teenager finds it humorous is because it would seem you would need a book that long to explain how women think. The following meme (next page) was popular on the internet and seems to symbolize the difference between men and women when they go to the mall.

Humor is best when it is encased in truth and for this reason the differences between how men and women approach purchasing, the things they need, will always be comical.

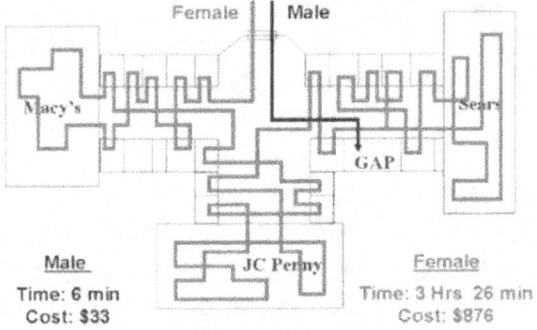

Mission: Go to Gap, Buy a Pair of Pants

Male
Time: 6 min
Cost: $33

Female
Time: 3 Hrs 26 min
Cost: $876

Women shop and Men Buy

Women shop and men buy, is a great and simple explanation to the difference between how men and women approach a purchase. Men are predominately logical, therefore, in a man's mind it would not make sense for him to spend so much needless time looking at stores or items that are not the desired item and the purpose for his visit to the store. Women are predominately emotional and will not be satisfied looking at only one item while visiting the store because the woman is more inclined to look for the more perfect item where the man will be satisfied with the first item found that fits the desired profile. Women will be thorough with their search and consider a multitude of variables during the deliberation process. Women shop, so you will want to provide an experience that the woman feels she is following her nature to explore all the viable options in order to make the best decision possible.

   A Master of the Sales Universe has a clear understanding of the feminine and masculine energies and applies that knowledge to a balanced sales approach. This approach considers the differences in perspective between men, women and married couples with dynamic results.

"Master a balance between masculine and feminine energies"

"Men are motivated when they feel needed while women are motivated when they feel cherished." John Gray

"Perfect kindness acts without thinking of kindness" Lao Tzu

"Masculine and feminine, vertical and horizontal" Piet Mondrian

10. THE LAW OF ACTION

Energy does not move without definite action

Action is required for any energy to move and nothing begins without something to initiate the process. The law of cause and effect starts at the law of action. The action will render the effect through initiating the movement of energy. The law of action is the call to move from thought vibration to manifestation and one cannot manifest without taking action. Thoughts alone are only the catalyst, the actions taken are the spark that trans-mutates an idea into existence. Knowing all about the laws of the universe and how to use that knowledge to create success in your selling career will only be possible with your action taking. YOU will want to make a commitment to take action, each day, to develop your desired results. Without action and applying your new found knowledge will not produce the desired results. How do you REALLY take action? Where do you start with taking action towards your career? To be a Master of the Sales Universe, it will require you to master action taking! The following steps are paramount in taking action:

1. A Commitment to Excellence

2. Create Detailed Plan of Action

3. Every Action Will Generate More Momentum Through Attraction (Attract through Action=Attraction)

4. Apply Energy and Invincible Determination

5. Stay Within Your Core Values to have best results

In my Pi Kappa Alpha fraternity house in the mid 1990's, we had a sign above the stairwell leading to the first floor. The sign said:

COMMITMENT TO EXCELLENCE

Below the sign were two painted hands where each of us would place our hands while walking down the stairway. I always looked forward to touching the sign because it reminded me about how my actions will reflect my commitment to being excellent. It really resonated with me and my hope is that it does for you too, because I'm going to give you a gift for taking action. I am instructing you to make your own sign and trace your hands to complete the required hand spaces, which you will use. Find a place to put it (mirror, vision board, office, locker, etc.) and have it visible. You will now use this sign as a symbol, which you will use to place your hands on every day to make your commitment to being excellent.

Commitment means you have obligated yourself to a certain standard and you are unwavering in your
position. Being *excellent* means: a high degree of good qualities; outstanding; prominent action taking; no excuse culture; means making decisions and following through to the end of the process; means no shortcuts; means your efforts and results are on a phenomenal level.

You have obligated yourself to an unwavering position of taking action to obtain YOUR highest degree of desired effect. You have a... <u>COMMITMENT TO EXCELLENCE</u>

**COMMITMENT
TO EXCELLENCE**

Remote controls have buttons. Push a button and get a desired result, but the channel won't change until you push the button. The commitment to excellence sign can be used like a button which you can push each day. After pushing the button, take at least one action, from your **Detailed Plan of Action**, that will get you closer to your desired effect. Putting your hands in the spaces will transfer energy and give you momentum to take action on the spot. Also, don't lose site of the "*excellent*" part of your *commitment*.

"*Action*," as [21]**Pablo Picasso** said, "*is the foundational key to all success*" and with it all great things start. Remember nothing moves (everything is energy) without an action taken to initiate the movement. In this chapter you will find that by having an **action trigger** to activate your commitment, you will be able to create momentum and consistency in your action taking. **<u>Each action you take is a step towards growth through excellence.</u>**

Additionally, each action you take creates a cause in the universe, that will accumulatively, render your desired effect (aspired goal). Constant movement towards your aspiration can be measured. In previous chapters you have learned about vibrational energy; how to magnetize your thought vibrations; that each existing thing has a polar spectrum; that each creation takes time to manifest; that manifestation requires masculine and feminine energies; that for every action there is an equal or opposite reaction. Action is required for any and all of the previous listed laws to occur.

Everything begins with the movement of energy. You can use continual movement (action) to create a momentum of energy to trans-mutate thought vibrational energy into its material equivalence in order to manifest your intently desired results. [22]**William Walker Atkinson**, the author of THOUGHT VIBRATIONS, writes in his timeless classic a concept that you should never forget. A concept that will change your life if you choose to unleash it into your habits and sales career. What is this concept you ask?

*"**Energy and invincible determination** – these two things will sweep away mightily barriers and will surmount the greatest obstacles. And yet, they must be used together. Energy without determination will go to waste."*

Where does will power come from? How will you sustain your constant efforts to attain your career aspirations? What actions can you take to see immediate results in your day-to-day efforts? If action is energy directionalized, where is your energy best invested each day?

What does invincible determination mean to you? If you made a decision to use invincible determination in your action taking, do you believe you can be prevented from achieving your desired results? What would be more important for you to do with your sales career than, making the decision to commit to being excellent and apply your energy, efforts and actions toward your defined goal or purpose?

My recommendation, when following these steps to action taking, is to ***Stay Within Your Core Values to have best results.*** Core values, are the human character traits that are most closely related to your belief system. Write down in your journal a list of character traits and choose 5 that you hold most sacred above all others. When you have identified your core values, you have a new way to interpret your commitment to excellence by looking through the lens of your core values. Do this before taking action because if the action you are taking is out of balance with your core values, it will not function properly. Imagine a toddler toy puzzle and you are forcing a square block into a round space. No matter how hard you try the cornered block won't fit into the space. This is the same for taking action on something that doesn't fit your core values. **Alignment is necessary for your overall happiness and success.**

Inaction is the polar opposite of action and it seems to be a popular choice for many. Why do you procrastinate or fail to take action when necessary? What obstacles prevent you from taking action? Do fear or doubts prevent you from taking action? Do you procrastinate from getting important items complete? Do you hold a grudge against someone? Are you having issues with forgiving someone who has wronged you in some way? Why would that matter to action taking?

First, fear or doubts grow in a garden without faith. Just as often, they develop from our programming (paradigms). You (and I) became programmed early in life from family, friends, teachers, neighbors, and so many others. The limitations and parameters that you believe are possible are your created paradigms. These paradigms represent the borders of your perceived possibilities. **Shakespeare** said of doubt, "*our doubts are traitors and make us lose the good we oft might by fearing to attempt*". Just remember that your energy goes where you focus your thought vibrations, so focus your energy in faith and possibilities and not in doubt or limitations.

Second, procrastination, that son of a bitch, comes from a lack of commitment. Excellence and procrastination are not related in any way unless you are talking about being excellent at procrastinating. Inaction exists when there is not enough energy focused on that item to create movement or to take action. Only when you are focused on achievement and being excellent while in the process, will you be in a vibrational frequency to make progress. Remember that the more you start taking action steps each day and progress begins to become visible, you will procrastinate less. It's exciting to see your results taking form.

Last, it is important to explore a subject that many of you will be surprised to find in this chapter, but I will make a case why it is more than relevant. The habit of forgiveness it is not that easy for some. Many hold their emotions locked away inside. There are people who have had their feelings hurt by others and are harboring those feelings without releasing that energy. Holding negative energy for people or situations can become a festering mess. This, I call, "forgiveness withheld". When you hold back your forgiveness to others, you are keeping dark and negative energy stored in your body. The accumulation of this negative energy can actually debilitate or hinder your ability to take action. Think of *forgiveness withheld* like constipation of your vibrational frequency or like big weeds growing in your mental garden. Forgiveness can create a vibrational frequency from which your energy is free and accessible because it is not being drained with negative energy. So, I recommend you take a serious look into forgiving all those you want to forgive. The act of forgiveness is more valuable for you personally as it is for the other party. The reason is connected to the release of the stored up negative energy that opens up the flow of energy to us. Action is energy initiated.

Becoming a Master of the Sales Universe will require you to also become a master of the law of action. [8]**Lao Tzu** said "*the journey of a thousand miles begins with a single step*", which exemplifies the law of action. Without this law, nothing initiates and stagnation exists. When this law is fully understood and adhered to, those applying it live in a world of possibilities, growth and increase.

"Master your action taking"

"Knowing is not enough; we must apply. Willing is not enough; we must do." Johann Wolfgang Van Goethe

"You may never know what results some of your action, but if you do nothing there will be no results." Mahatma Gandhi

"Thinking will not overcome fear, but action will."   W Clement Stone

11. THE LAW OF CORRESPONDENCE

Connection exists between conscious and subconscious

If you were to look in a textbook, at a spectrum of sound wavelengths you would discover that there are sound waves your ears cannot hear, however, they do exist regardless. The same applies with light wavelengths, as there are spectrums of light not visible to the human eye, but they exist whether your eyes can see them or not. There is much you cannot see, but yet it still exists. There is a spiritual world outside of your human senses that exists whether you see it or believe it, or not. The way in which we can connect to that spiritual world is through our super-conscious (subconscious) mind and our super-conscious mind is our connection to the universal source.

Your connection with the spiritual world is parallel to the physical world and will reflect, like a mirror, the content of the super-conscious. Meaning there is a correspondence between your inner world and the outer world. The beauty of this law is that the outer world you live and experience will reflect your inner world of thought vibrational frequency. Where you are focusing your vibrational energy will reflect in your outer world experiences. What is happening in your outer world will affect your inner thoughts. Your inner turmoil creates outer experience turmoil. Your inner peace will reflect to those whom come into contact with you. Conclusion, you can apply the law of correspondence to observe your outworld in order to make changes to your inner world and subsequently, you can change your inner world (your thought vibrations) to affect your outer world results.

This law provides you with observable results, which you can take action to alter your desired vision and it will free you from the blame-game forever. Mastering the law of correspondence will supply you with unending ways to improve your results (both inside and out) and liberate you from empowering others with your sovereign power.

"Thought and character are one, and as character can only manifest and discover itself through environment and circumstance, the outer conditions of a person's life will always be found to be harmoniously related to his inner state. This does not mean that a man's circumstances at any given time are an indication of his entire character, but that those circumstances are so intimately connected with some vital thought-element within himself that,

for the time being, they are indispensable to his development."

24 James Allen

How can you learn to improve with the law of correspondence? Everything happening in your life is a direct result of your choices, thoughts and habits and therefore can be adjusted to change the results. The correspondence occurs from the mental, physical to the spiritual levels hence the phrase "*As above, so below; As within, so without*".

When you look in the mirror you are looking at a reflection of yourself and when you go into your home its condition is a reflection of how you live. When you are making a sales presentation, your inner world is reflected to your customers through physical expression. Go back to chapter 1 and recall how, vibrational energy shows up in your **tone of voice**, **body language**, **eye contact** and even your **nonverbal communication**. The reason it shows up in your physicality and your tonality is because it is a reflection of how you feel inside (your vibrational frequency). Your thought vibrations will correspond to your physical body language. *Changing how you feel will also change your body language.* Slouched posture and shifty eyes correspond with low energy and low trustworthiness, hence others observing that person will feel that low or negative energy frequency.

    Having a positive vibrational broadcast starts from your thought vibrations. Grateful thought vibrations will render positive vibrations to the outer world, so if you are feeling blessed to be alive and you are excited for the opportunities of the day the corresponding result will be that the vibrational frequency you are broadcasting will transfer that sentiment to the outer environment. Your co-workers, customers and anyone else you encounter will want to be on your frequency because it's contagious and desirable to feel good. For years I have claimed that happiness starts on the inside and fills the center of your being and people who don't realize that are trying to fill that hole with all kinds of outer world things, but they can't satisfy it because happiness is within. *As within, so without.* What can you do to create an internal happiness? If you are mentally in a frequency of joy how will that affect the rapport you create with your customers?

    Recently I was travelling and connecting through the Phoenix airport. I sat down to have something to eat and drink before my next flight. A server came to the table with a menu and I began to analyze every item, looking for the most exciting option to eat. I asked the waitress for an item on the menu and she said that it wasn't available. Next, I asked for a Reuben sandwich with fries (as it advertised in the menu). She replied that we have the sandwich, but no fries. I was disappointed and decided not to order food only a draft beer. A few minutes later I heard a different waiter two tables over giving a wonderful description of some of the same dishes I had been looking at on the menu, but the way he was describing the food made me second guess my food abstinence. A moment later TJ (the waiter) came by to ask if I needed anything. I told him what had happened and he said, "we will have some fries in a few minutes and when your plate is ready, I'll bring it out to you". From there I observed TJ running circles around the other servers, making jokes like "SOLD!" when someone would order something off the menu and his energy and love for his job was contagious. After enough observation, I asked TJ to speak with me for a moment. I said, "I am writing a book related to sales and my observation is that you are operating at a higher level than any of your co-workers. Where does that come from?" He told me that he had been working there for 7 years and his previous work was hard labor and long hours. He added that he loves the hours he works and feels he has a life outside of work, but when he is working, he wants to be the best he can be and from doing so makes him happy. Our conversation ended with him saying, "if you've come through the Phoenix airport a few times, its likely I've been your server". TJ is a great example of someone's inner world (energy, dedication and gratitude) reflecting their outer world. TJ's grateful frequency and commitment to excellence was as clear and definite as tuning into a radio station. He was dialed in, I took notice and ordered food with him where the first server had been unsuccessful and unconvincing.

It is well known that tree roots must grow as large as the visible tree in order to give it structural support. **Service first vibrational frequency** and genuine **gratitude** are the roots of this tree of sales success. *As above, so below.* If you want your money tree to grow big and healthy you need that your roots are big and healthy too.

There is a correspondence with blaming others for your misfortunes and a life of powerless regret. It is easy to not accept full responsibility for your life and everything in it, however, the law of correspondence (which is an inarguable law) tells you it is your responsibility. It is easy for one to fail and cast the blame on a person, place or thing or anything other than themselves. However, when you choose to make an excuse and not choose to take responsibility you are surrendering your power and giving it away.

"I would have won, but the winner is friends with the office manager"

"it's not my fault, they started it"

"It wasn't my responsibility to do that"

When you blame something, you are giving that something your power. Your reason for failing is because someone else did something? You are saying that you don't have control over your life and that someone else does. If you don't have control of your life through your choices, then that means someone else does. *As within, so without.* Excuses from the inside will affect everything on the outside like a sticky glue. Nothing seems easy or effortless because your energy and power have been surrendered. It is convenient to accept praise when you are successful and reject responsibility when you fail, however, it is counter-productive in the long term. Only when you can take responsibility for all results, positive or negative, can you maximize your energy and retain your personal power. I believe that taking responsibility directly corresponds to self-esteem and humility and embracing responsibility for your results will empower you beyond any other habit. Energy is stored within you and waiting to be implemented towards your next desired result, when you give that energy away through the blame-game you will inevitably not have enough energy to trans-mutate your most important projects and you won't feel you have the power to change the situation because someone else has been transferred your power.

Masters of the Sales Universe do not give away their power and they do not point at others when they fail, they always take responsibility. Mental management, protecting your thoughts and words, and taking full responsibility for your sales career will all correspond to development, growth and overall satisfaction in your vocation. Begin today with your own culture of "NO EXCUSES" and "I take responsibility for everything in my life and career", because when you do the evidence will be visible everywhere around you.

"Master your inner world for best results in your outer world"

"The law of correspondence says your outer world is a mirror of your inner world. Your outer world corresponds to your inner world. Your outer world of your relationships-especially with your children and spouse-simply corresponds to how you

feel about yourself, how you're doing"
Brian Tracy

"If you want to awaken all of humanity, then awaken all of yourself. If you want to eliminate the suffering in the world, then eliminate all that is dark and negative in yourself. Truly, the greatest gift you have to give is that of your own self-transformation"
Lao Tzu

12. The Law of Connected Universe

Everything in the universe is connected through energy and origin

In the first chapter you learned how the entire universe is energy and everything in it. All energy vibrates at specific quantified frequencies. In this final chapter you will understand that because everything is energy and is comprised of the same material, at a quantum level, that everything and everyone is connected. This connection of all things is the 'source' of the universe. The 'source' is an energy field of timeless knowledge, a connection to the divine which has been discovered can be used to connect your imagination with the infinite. Thomas Edison attributed his rocking chair meditations with his connecting to the infinite source of energy. He labeled this source of knowledge the 'Infinite Mind', where inspiration would be revealed to him in the form of solutions through intuition. In this chapter you will learn about this infinite source of knowledge and how it is connected to all things, how that connection brings us all closer together, how connecting with the source can lead to inspiration through intuition and how intuition can be developed as a skill through this connected universe. Intuition, when developed, can be a powerful tool of a Master of the Sales Universe.

This Universal Oneness that connects us all together, once recognized, can become a source of energy for your vocation. When you lean towards self-esteem and humility and combine that frequency with the recognition that all things are connected, you can harness that sentiment in all actions you take. In a sales environment there is not just a sales team involved. There are typically many others working in the same office that are assisting the sales team. There are custodian workers, hostesses, office assistants and office managers and the list, goes on. When you apply the law of the connected universe, you realize that we are all a part of something bigger than ourselves and because of this we can act accordingly with all of the people we interact with during our office hours.

Having this mindset towards all those you work with will broadcast a frequency that is contagious to receive. Like the spokes of a wheel, all those involved have a contribution to your success and you will receive an equal measure to what you give to each of them. This is leadership through recognition of contribution and the effects will render a wonderful work environment, especially if everyone can buy into that philosophy through a shared sentiment and flowing vibrational frequency. In other words, do on to your co-workers as you would have them do to you. Start with saying hi and offering a smile to all those you work with each day by remembering that we are all connected. Their feelings and sentiments are relative to your vibrational frequency and the cause and effect results can shift a sales team into a different gear.

In [23]**Dr. Steven Covey's** classic, THE SEVEN HABITS OF HIGHLY EFFECTIVE PEOPLE, the sixth habit is Synergize. Synergy is a culmination of efforts where the whole is recognized to be greater than its individual parts, and where greater results can be achieved through the combined efforts of the team working together than each working individually towards the same goal. The law of the connected universe is parallel to this habit and is the influencer in the process. To synergize is to create through a focused action energy to trans-mutate a stronger result through the contributions of many. The ego and low self-esteem vibrations are not conducive to synergy and synergy is required to create great sales success. No one is an island and no one makes a success on their own. Synergy is key to a success flow of energy, so you want to keep that in mind as another reason to keep your self-esteem high and your humility on display to nurture the connection you have with all those you spend so many hours a day with.

I have worked with hundreds of different sales characters over the years. Many have questionable motivations for their sales approach. To consider your customer an enemy or a win-lose sales dynamic is the antithesis of genuine customer appreciation and living with this recognition of a connected universe.

Many times, I have brought up the love vibration concept and I will end the book with the same mantra. A service first sales approach is in alignment with the law of connected universe and for this reason it works so smoothly and without extreme effort because it is a frequency broadcast. This broadcasting can become a habit that you bring to your customers everyday like a shining gift. The genuine warmth of your love vibration will connect with your customer producing an effect that allows you to not have to speak so much or work so hard, in regards in creating rapport and participation. Masters of the Sales

Universe will see each day as an opportunity to connect, communicate and persuade through this energy field that connects us all together.

The law of connected universe explains that because everything is connected there are ways to super consciously connect with the source. [25]**Napolean Hill** referred to this, in *The Sixth Sense* chapter of THINK AND GROW RICH, as the Universal Mind. The Universal Mind is a connected flow of energy consciousness, which your imagination can access through your, sixth sense. The sixth sense connects to a universal frequency of knowledge, which you can use for guidance and inspiration. Some people call this "going with your gut" or intuition. I believe that intuition is a cause of the connected universe effect and is the provider of universal knowledge through our connected oneness. Therefore, intuition can become a skill which you can develop and increase over time. How helpful would it be to your life and your career to be ever increasing your intuitional skills? Have you ever listened to your intuition with great results? How can you develop more use of your intuition? Is it possible that you are being given signals and ignoring them? How can you be in-tune with your intuition?

Your mental faculties include perception, memory, will power, reason, imagination and intuition. The last two are directly related to the law of connected universe. Both imagination and intuition can extrapolate from the universal mind to bring forth inspiration to anyone connected and at a moment's notice. Have you ever had a flash of inspiration? Have you ever woken up to write down an idea that just came into your mind? The superconscious mind is your connection to the universal source and depending on your brain wave status during sleep, you can enter a dreamlike state where the two worlds meet.

Thomas Edison famously used this dream state to develop many of the inspired inventions he created. There is a statue of Thomas Edison at the Edison Ford Winter Estate in Fort Meyers, Florida. If you look closely, has metal balls in his grip. This is because Edison would fall asleep with large metal balls for the purpose to wake him suddenly to which he would write down anything that came to his mind.

How can you implement this concept to your sales career? Carrying metal balls around may not be the best strategy, but you can ask for inspiration right before you go to sleep and take note of the first things that come to your mind when you awaken. You can meditate to connect to the source. You can sit in complete silence; which gives your mind a chance to think less; which allows the whisper of intuition to speak to you. Giving your superconscious mind instructions to solve a problem while you are sleeping is another. Remember that no problem can exist without a solution, inspire your superconscious mind to solve any situation through imagination and all while you sleep.

    Apply this to your career in sales. How would meditating about your day bring perspective to your daily action taking? Could you make a small list of what you want to take action on and reflect about it at the end of the day? Would you focus on the positive or negative aspects regarding your production? How would meditating before work put you into focus for the day? How would giving your subconscious mind problems to solve during the night create better results? Why is it so important to know that every problem has a solution and that there is collective knowledge that is accessible to you to solve any problem? If you accept that every problem has a solution and that every solution is accessible, how will you apply that knowledge to your sales career? Is there any obstacle in your path that cannot be overcome?

In the eternal book [24]*AS A MAN THINKETH*, **James Allen** describes that understanding these universal laws is understanding that everything is connected through these laws, "*Law, not confusion, is the dominating principle in the universe; justice, not injustice, is the soul and substance of life; and righteousness, not corruption, is the moulding and moving force in the spiritual government of the world. This being so, man has but to right himself to find that the universe is right; and during the process of putting himself right he will find that as he alters his thoughts towards things and other people, things and other people will alter towards him.*"

Masters of the Sales Universe apply the knowledge of the connected universe to perceive the world through mental, physical and spiritual expression, all while being in balance with the universal laws. The mastery of this law will have great effect on your personal and business relationships; your self-esteem and humility; your ability to create through imagination and intuition; and your ability to ultimately connect to the universal mind in order to access solutions that are outside of your thought vibration's parameters. When you broadcast a vibrational frequency of gratitude and apply your mastery of these irrefutable laws, you will forever change your life and your sales career to heights that only you can express through your action taking!

Congratulations, you now know how to become a Master of the Sales Universe. How will YOU apply these laws and this knowledge into YOUR sales career and life? The answer is for YOU to create...

"Master your connection to the source through humility"

"You are never alone. You are connected to everyone." Amit Ray

"You and I are all as much continuous with the physical universe as a wave is continuous with the ocean." Alan Watts

"Each person that you meet is an aspect of yourself, clamoring for love." Eric Micha'el Leventhal

"And he is before all things, and in Him all things consist." Colossians 1:17

"as above, so below, so within, as the universe, so the soul" **Hermes Trismegistus**

APPENDIX:

Master of the Sales Universe

(1) Dr. Emoto – 2004 – THE HIDDEN MESSAGES IN WATER

(2) Robert Perkins & Amy Blumenthal – November 23, 2015 USC Voice tone analysis with algorithm study Science News

(3) Grimal & Maman – 1981 - THE TAO OF SOUND

(4) Albert Mehrabian – 1967 Communication Rule 7/38/55

(5) Chris Shryak – 2018 Performance with Power

(6) Deepak Chopra – 2015 - The Law of Giving and Receiving

(7) Fitzgerald – 1852 - SOLOMON'S SEAL

(8) Lao Tzu – TAO TE CHING *English translation

(9) Sequoia National Park

(10) Forbes Magazine – 2020 #616 John Morris article

(11) Gandhi – Goodquotes.com

(12) Echart Tolle – 2008 A New Earth: Awakening to your Life's Purpose

(13) Marcus Aurelius – MEDITATIONS – 1747 - The Commentaries of the Emperor Marcus Aurelius – Translated by James Thompson

(14) Banglor University – July 10, 2019 Using self-talk article medicalxpress.com

(15) Lucretius - ON THE NATURE OF THINGS – 2008 – Translated by Sir Ronald Melville

(16) Jim Kwik thermometer/stat

(17) Milanovich Mccuny –1996 - THE LIGHT SHALL SET YOU FREE

(18) Sarah Allen - 2002 - Effects of Father Involvement: Summary of the Research Evidence – Newletter of the Father Involvement Initiative

(19) Erica Komisar – 2017 – BEING THERE: WHY MOTHERHOOD IN THE FIRST THREE YEARS MATTERS

(20) Chris Voss – 2016 – NEVER SPLIT THE DIFFERENCE

(21) Pablo Picasso – Goodreads.com

(22) William Walker Atkinson – 1906 – THOUGHT VIBRATION: OR THE LAW OF ATTRACTION IN THE THOUGHT WORLD

(23) Dr Covey – 1989 - THE 7 HABITS OF HIGHLY EFFECTIVE PEOPLE

(24) James Allen - 1903 - AS A MAN THINKETH

(25) Napolean Hill – 1937 – THINK AND GROW RICH

www.ingramcontent.com/pod-product-compliance
Lightning Source LLC
Chambersburg PA
CBHW071412210526
45465CB00001B/356